BETWEEN TWO CULTURES

BETWEEN

TWO CULTURES

A PHOTOGRAPHER AMONG THE INUIT

MARIA TIPPETT

WITH PHOTOGRAPHS BY
CHARLES GIMPEL

VIKING

VIKING

Published by the Penguin Group

Penguin Books Canada Ltd, 10 Alcorn Avenue, Toronto, Ontario, Canada, M4V 3B2

Penguin Books Ltd, 27 Wrights Lane, London W8 5TZ, England

Viking Penguin, a division of Penguin Books USA Inc., 375 Hudson Street, New York, New York, 10014, USA

Penguin Books Australia Ltd, Ringwood, Victoria, Australia

Penguin Books (NZ) Ltd, 182-190 Wairau Road, Auckland 10, New Zealand

Penguin Books Ltd, Registered Offices: Harmondsworth, Middlesex, England

First published 1994

10 9 8 7 6 5 4 3 2 1

Book design by Counterpunch/Linda Gustafson
Printed in Hong Kong

Canadian Cataloguing in Publication Data
Tippett, Maria, 1944–
Between two cultures: a photographer among the Inuit 1958 to 1968
ISBN 0-670-85243-0
1. Gimpel, Charles. 2. Inuit – Canada.*
3. Photographers – Great Britain – Biography.
i. Gimpel, Charles. ii. Title.
TR140.G5T5 1994   770'.92   C93-094707-X

British Library Cataloguing in Publication Data Available

for

Kay Gimpel, Fran Gundry,

and

Sue Wagner

CONTENTS

CHARLES GIMPEL AND I arrived in Cape Dorset in 1958 only a month apart. He was northbound on the HBC vessel *M. V. Rupertsland* and I southbound on the government ice-breaker the C.D. Howe. We did not meet.

I was returning from a two-year posting in north Baffin Island (Clyde River), where I had been Officer-in-Charge at a Radiosonde weather station. Having graduated from the Ontario College of Art in 1954 with a desire to paint the Arctic landscape, I found it necessary to obtain my diploma as a Meteorological Technician in order to secure my passage north. Travel into Canada's Arctic was difficult in the 1950s for anyone without some connection with the fledgling government of the day, or with an agency like the Hudson's Bay Company, the RCMP, or the missions.

Charles was an oddity in the Arctic, not so much because he was a colourful eccentric (there were a number of these), but rather because he represented a unique contrast to the conventional southerner of the time, few as they were. Unlike the teachers, traders, or missionaries, Charles was an urbane individual from a sophisticated world little known to non-Native people, let alone to the Inuit themselves. Indeed, Charles was seen as something of a character, a clown of sorts, who masked his awe of the North with an exaggerated stance – behaviour out of character, I would suggest, with the persona he exhibited in London among his art collector clients and colleagues. His was a complex character, and he often spoke of the enjoyment he received from his disparate identities as genteel Mayfair art dealer and chronicler of the Inuit of the day.

Charles took great pleasure in photographing the people and the landscapes of the North, exhibiting an unremitting enthusiasm for his subject matter. He liked the company of the Inuit and derived special satisfaction in his experiences "in country," despite the genuinely arduous nature of his journeys by dog team. Each time he returned to Cape Dorset he brought with him copies of his photos from previous trips, a gesture that not only was appreciated by those he photographed but also guaranteed him receptive subjects for subsequent shoots. Too few photographers had this common good sense, and it stood him in good favour.

FOREWORD

An abiding interest in the arts of other cultures contributed to Charles's fascination with all things Arctic, and especially with the changing face of the North. He headed a list of contemporaries from many walks of life who have found real pleasure, excitement and gratification in the challenge of the Arctic, particularly at a time in their lives when they had not expected to find such a release from the dictates of their chosen professions. Some have since painted or written eloquently of their experiences or simply expanded their own horizons as Charles expanded his.

We travelled together on only a few occasions, I the young aspiring artist becoming ever more involved in the art of the Inuit, and he the urbane, witty London dealer with the fascinating background in wartime espionage. The latter was a topic he was careful to avoid, given the pain he obviously suffered during the course of the war years. What few comments I recall hearing were during those times we were weather-bound on the land, with the time and inclination to recollect. He never mentioned the many awards I subsequently learned he had received.

The few remaining Inuit elders who knew Charles remember him with affection and respect as that Kadloona (white man) called "Ukjuk" (bearded seal, because of the tufts of hair he sported on his cheeks). His memory will live on among future generations as the man who took all those pictures and gave his Inuit friends reason to laugh at his warmth and antics.

Terry Ryan

West Baffin Eskimo Co-operative

Cape Dorset

I FIRST LEARNED about Charles Gimpel's interest in the Arctic while looking at the work of modern British artists at the Gimpel Fils Gallery in London, England. Charles, Kay, and Peter Gimpel had, I soon discovered, done more than support modernist British artists of the calibre of Ben Nicholson, Barbara Hepworth, and Henry Moore, theirs was the first European gallery to exhibit Inuit carvings as works of art rather than as curios or museum artefacts. Nor was this all. Five years after the Gallery's seminal exhibition of Inuit art in 1953, Charles Gimpel made the first of six trips to the Canadian Eastern Arctic. Over the course of the next ten years, 1958 to 1968, he selected carvings, drawings, and prints for exhibition in Switzerland and France as well as in England. He travelled in 1964 by dog sled to view the stone cairns or Inuksuiit at the acropolis of the Canadian Eastern Arctic, Inuksugasalik Point. And during every trip he indulged in his favourite pastime – taking photographs.

Gimpel's photographs were initially used as a backdrop for the display of Inuit sculpture. Then in 1964 the Smithsonian Institution in Washington, D.C. put the photographs themselves on display at venues throughout the United States and Canada.

When I first clapped my eyes on Gimpel's photographs in 1991, they were hanging on the walls of his widow's South Kensington mews house. I was immediately impressed by their freshness, by their artistic merit, and by their remarkable insight into the Inuit predicament. The erosion of the Native way of life, due to the onslaught of southern Canada's social, cultural, and political traditions and its technological know-how, had caught the Inuit "Between Two Cultures."

The rest of the photographs, Kay Gimpel informed me, were stored in the basement of the Gimpel Fils Gallery in Mayfair. After viewing them, my colleague Gloria Carnevali and I arranged an exhibition, *The Inuit World As Seen by Charles Gimpel,* at the Clare Hall Art Gallery at Cambridge University. The response to the exhibition, which opened in May 1992, was so favourable that I decided to make the photographs more widely known by presenting them in book form.

From the moment I began preparing Charles Gimpel's photographs for publication,

I incurred many debts. There were the resourceful librarians at the Scott Polar Research Institute in Cambridge, where I was helped, too, by the distinguished geographer Terence Armstrong. Keith Hart introduced me to the field of anthropological studies. The writer and artist James Houston generously shared his memories of Charles Gimpel with me. Joan Schwartz, Peter Robertson, and other archivists at the National Archives of Canada and the National Library of Canada in Ottawa, Virginia Watt of the Canadian Handicrafts Guild in Montreal, and Anne Morton at the Hudson's Bay Company Archives in Winnipeg gave me their assistance. At the Gimpel Fils Gallery in London the late Derek Keen unearthed documents and clippings from the gallery's archives. Kay Gimpel made great efforts to provide me with more negatives, prints, and valuable manuscript material in her home, and my use of them there was also facilitated by Brigid Ferry.

I did not expect to find much more information to add to my knowledge of the photographs when I arrived on Baffin Island in June 1993. But to my surprise and joy I found many of Charles's friends: Abe Okpik and Joanasie Salomonie in Iqaluit; Kov Parr, Mikkigak Pee, Pitaloosie and Pauta Saila, Simeonie Kopapik, Kananginak, and Iyola King-watsiak in Cape Dorset. With the help of an interpreter, Katauga Saila of Cape Dorset, these elders identified many of the people in the photographs. They did this by noting the pattern on the sleeve of a parka, by viewing a photograph from the side and thus "finding" the profile of a face, and by looking at the print from the back in order to give the image a three-dimensional quality. In Pangnirtung Simon and Sarah Shaimaiyuk, Atsayuk Etaungat, Paulosi Angmarlik, Towkie Maniapik, and Ikeeloak Komoatuk told me, with the help of Ooleepeeka Nakashuk, about life in that community during the 1950s, and Yves Bossé gave me a comfortable place to stay. And in Cape Dorset Terry Ryan, who runs the West Baffin Eskimo Co-operative, and his assistant Jimmy Manning shared their wide knowledge of Inuit art with me. All of these people were helpful with their sometimes moving and frequently comical accounts of Charles Gimpel. They deserve my warmest thanks for making my visit to Baffin Island so rewarding.

During the preparation of *Between Two Cultures* for publication I was supported, once again, by Penguin Books in Toronto, particularly by my editor, Jackie Kaiser, copy-editor, Mary Adachi, and superb designer, Linda Gustafson. Renee Wissink, Terry Ryan, and Ian Whitaker pulled the thorns out of the first draft of the manuscript. And John MacDonald of the Research Centre in Igloolik provided linguistic assistance. To all of these people, as well as to Peter Clarke who read several versions of the text at our cottage on Bowen Island in British Columbia while he was engaged in writing a book of a very different kind for Penguin, and to my friends Kay Gimpel, Fran Gundry, and Sue Wagner, to whom this book is dedicated, I am most grateful for their friendship, their patience, and for their support. Finally the Smuts Memorial Fund, the British Academy, and my Cambridge college, Clare Hall, deserve special acknowledgment for the part they played in bringing this book to fruition.

Maria Tippett, Cambridge, England

AUTHOR'S NOTE

Since the invention of photography in 1839, photographs have, for the most part, been subordinated to the written word. I have attempted to redress this situation. By prefacing each section with an epigraph based on excerpts from Gimpel's journals, lectures, and essays and by following this with my own commentary, I have sought to avoid overloading the captions accompanying the photographs. Every effort has, however, been made to locate, date, and identify the people and the activity taking place in each photograph.

I have employed English-Canadian uses of Inuk for a single person, Innuk for two, and Inuit for the plural. I have retained commonplace names as they were used by non-Natives in the 1950s and 1960s, indicating, where applicable, the current name in brackets, e.g. Sugluk (Salluit). I have corrected Gimpel's misspellings in the epigraphs. Finally it should be noted that all unannotated interviews were conducted by the author on Baffin Island in June of 1993.

AN AMATEUR OF
THE ARCTIC

As for my brief biography: I am a Frenchman, married to a Canadian living in London. Third generation

of art dealers. My brother and I have galleries in London and Zurich specializing in modern painting

and sculpture. I have made several trips to the Canadian Eastern Arctic, taken many thousands of

photographs up there and hope to have a country house in the near future on Baffin Island. I could

perhaps call myself an amateur of the Arctic but the Eskimo seem to be more precise and have

christened me "Oui Oui Ukjuq" the French bearded seal.[1]

Charles Gimpel, 20 November 1962

Charles gimpel wrote about himself and about how he was perceived as an "amateur" of the Arctic with a great deal of wit and insight. Yet the photographs taken by this "elegant, robust, red-cheeked man" who was "sometimes . . . very French, [and] sometimes very English" convey his Arctic experiences even more poignantly.[2] In fact, soon after I began my research into the history of Arctic photography, I realized that I had stumbled upon a seminal collection of photographs that encompassed, yet went well beyond, the subjects and stylistic approaches of those Arctic photographers before him.

Exploration photographers at the middle of the nineteenth century such as Amos Bonsall, an officer on board the privately funded American expedition commanded by Elisha Kent Kane from 1853 to 1855, and Thomas Mitchell, who accompanied Britain's Nares Expedition during the mid-1870s, produced photographic documentaries using the daguerreotype process and wet glass plate negatives respectively. However, the first artistic expedition to the Eastern Arctic was led by the American artist-photographer William Bradford. When the *Panther* reached the west coast of Greenland in 1869, Bradford was overwhelmed by the luminosity of the "novel, impressive, astonishing" snow and ice forms.[3] His photographs of icebergs in particular served like picture postcards to show the folk back home how terrifying was the terrain above the taiga forests. They also complemented the landscape paintings of ice-locked ships that Caspar David Friedrich, Sir Edwin Landseer, and other painters were producing from their imagination for the European public. Whether paintings or photographs, these sometimes terrifying yet highly imaginative works fit squarely into what has been called the Arctic Sublime.

Gimpel felt no need to dwell upon the seasonally hostile features of the northern landscape in his photographs. He knew that Winnipeg, the childhood home of his wife, Kay Moore, lying far south of the tundra, could experience equally cold and harsh temperatures, though of shorter duration, during the long winter months. Indeed his first trip to the Arctic was made in the late summer when the exposed surfaces of the smooth rocks were covered with grey-green reindeer moss and their rough crevices filled with clumps of

Previous page: Self-portrait, Charles Gimpel, Point Enukso, 4 April 1968

scrub willow and purple saxifrage. This is not to suggest that Gimpel ignored the shorefast ice forms, the moving packs of sea ice, the white-outs, and the lofty icebergs when, on his later trips, snow and ice did prevail. In fact "Charles's mind and eye," according to the artist and writer James Houston, "seemed to be in tune with the broad stretches of open tundra, the mountains and ice-strewn sea."[4] The monochromatic snow and icescapes — with their alternating sense of depth and scale, with their absence of boundary or horizon, and with their wraith-like mirages — allowed Gimpel to explore abstract form and space in much the same way as the modernist artists at his London gallery, the Gimpel Fils.

While William Bradford was establishing a vogue for photographing the so-called barren Arctic wastelands during the second half of the nineteenth century, amateur photographers like James L. Cotter, George Simpson McTavish, Geraldine Moodie, and Captain James Mutch began pointing their cameras at the region's indigenous people. Cotter and McTavish did this from their Hudson's Bay Company posts at Moose Factory and Little Whale River; Moodie from a makeshift studio on board the *Arctic* in Hudson Bay; and Mutch from Kekerten, a whaling station located on an island off the east coast of Baffin Island.

Photographs of the Inuit remained little more than exotic curiosities, however, until 1883 when Franz Boas, the German geographer and ethnologist, took a camera with him to what was then called Baffinland. There he photographed the landscape and the Inuit camps. Five years later when the Smithsonian Institution published an acccount of his trip in *The Central Eskimo*[5] the accompanying plates, according to the captions under them, were based on photographs taken on Baffin Island. Yet most of his film had been lost during the trip and what remained, in the view of one scholar, was "barely 'adequate'" for reproduction.[6] Therefore two years after returning to Germany Boas and his servant, Wilhelm Weike, donned the caribou clothing they had acquired in the Arctic, assumed several poses relating to seal-hunting, and had themselves photographed in Hülsenbeck's studio in Minden. After an artist had added snowscape backgrounds to the prints, the photographs were

Charles Gimpel, circa 1962,
photographed by Anders Holmquist

ready to be engraved onto plates.[7] No one immediately caught on to the fact that caribou clothing, snow and ice, harpoons, and seals stood proxy for *real* Inuit men in this first major ethnographic study of the Inuit peoples.

Though Charles Gimpel judiciously cropped his photographs and, with the help of his technician Miss Deste, transformed his negatives into superb prints, he never took such liberties. But he didn't have to. The Canadian Eastern Arctic was not as inaccessible in the 1950s as it had been in the early 1880s. (Boas made several attempts to return yet failed to obtain the necessary financial backing.) Just as Boas had thought it vital "to save what can yet be saved" of the Inuit way of life, so Gimpel knew that he was in the Arctic at a critical time.[8] This prompted him to make a pictorial record of tool making, seal and duck hunting, fox trapping, and fishing for arctic char. It spurred him to undergo the long and arduous trip in 1964 to Inuksugasalik Point, where under severe weather conditions he, Joanasie Salomonie, and Kov Parr photographed, measured, and mapped several stone cairns or Inuksuiit whose number totalled over one hundred.

Following the monumental publication of Boas's *The Central Eskimo*, adventurers and explorers like Agnes Deans Cameron, Julian W. Bilby, Philip H. Godsell, and Vilhjalmur Stefansson seldom failed to include photographs of the Arctic in their best-selling books or, if they were lecturing, show lantern slides during their public talks.[9] This was because illustrations gave authority to their text or talk; they entertained and they enticed. Visual documentation of what many perceived to be the soon-to-vanish "Eskimo" also provided their publications and their performances with a sense of urgency. But above all, photographs of the vast Arctic landscape and its exotic inhabitants offered evidence of the physical prowess of the person who had taken them. For unlike the ill-fated members of the Franklin expedition, whose disappearance off the west coast of King William Island during their search for the Northwest Passage in 1845 turned romantic adventure into grim reality, these author-adventurers and explorers had miraculously survived. That this was due to the assistance of their Inuit guides, whose example Franklin's 128 men chose to ignore, went largely unacknowledged. To present the indigenous peoples of the Arctic as superb cartographers, navigators, and hunters rather than, in line with conventional thinking, as "happy-go-lucky, sporting folk, affectionate to their families, [and] friendly and generous to all members of their community"[10] would have diminished the author's own heroic accomplishment.

Gimpel felt no need to travel to the Arctic in order to undergo what by the early twentieth century had become for many adventurers a rite of passage. He had done that during the Second World War. Before the hostilities began, Gimpel completed his military service with the cavalry in North Africa. (Before that he studied political science at the University of Paris, for whom he played rugby, and art history at the Beaux Arts in the same city.) Conscripted as an "other rank" in the tank regiment in 1939, Gimpel was in the retreat from Belgium, escaped from Dunkirk in 1940, then joined the Resistance. There he rose to the rank of Major and took Circle as a code name. Kay Moore had come to Europe in the mid 1930s from Winnipeg to study history at the Sorbonne in Paris. At the outbreak of the war she moved to London, was employed by Special Operations Executive, then became a liaison officer for the Free French. She "ran" her future husband until, following a series of spectacular escapes, Charles was arrested by the Gestapo in January of 1944. Gimpel spent the rest of the war in Buchenwald, Auschwitz, and then in Flossenburg. (He bore tattoo number 185663 on his left arm until the day he died.)

Following his war service, for which he was awarded the Legion d'honneur and the Compagnon de la Libération, among many other honours, Charles and his brother Peter set up the Gimpel Fils gallery in London. It was a memorial to their father who had died in Neuengamme concentration camp after his arrest for work in the Resistance. Founded in Paris in 1889 by their Alsatian grandfather, the gallery was initially part of the gilded age dealing with such luminaries as Mary Cassatt and Renoir, then with Picasso and Matisse. Charles and Peter continued this tradition by re-establishing contact with the gallery's Continental artists and, more importantly, by making room for the post-war generation of British painters and sculptors which included Ben Nicholson and Barbara Hepworth.

Thanks to his torture by the Gestapo, Charles did not enjoy the best of health following his incarceration. As he reminded Kay shortly before his death in 1973, he had been "on borrowed time since 1944."[11] Moreover he abhorred the cold. A photograph of Gimpel at Point Enukso shows him to be in great discomfort. This is not to suggest, however, that Charles's visits to the Canadian Arctic lacked a sense of adventure. According to James Houston, who accompanied Gimpel on his first excursion to the inland Inuit camps, "there was no Arctic trip he would not take; he welcomed risks on the bad ice, when dog-team travelling was at its worst."[12] And in the view of Charles's Inuk companion and interpreter, Joanasie Salomonie, with whom he later travelled to Inuksugasalik Point, "everything we would do, he tried it all."

Gimpel's initial interest in the Arctic was aroused when a friend, writing from a remote outpost in Newfoundland just after the war, told him: "you would love it out here for a while – great spaces and silences and a simple way of life are the keynotes."[13] The Arctic life certainly was simple compared with how Charles lived on the other side of the Atlantic. Most of his time was spent running galleries in London and Zurich and after 1969 in New York. With the help of his brother Peter, Kay, whom he married in August 1945, and eventually their eldest son René, Charles visited artists' studios, attended private and public exhibitions, and hobnobbed with British, American, and European art critics and gallery officials. During the summer months Charles and Kay attended the Venice Biennale where they were frequently the guests of the renowned American art collector Peggy Guggenheim. Every other year they travelled to Canada and the United States. And if there was time left over for a vacation, they spent it with their two sons in the fortified village of Ménerbes in Provence where they had made a home out of a former presbytery dating from the sixteenth century. After his first operation for cancer in 1970 Charles escaped to Ivy Cottage at Cretingham in Suffolk for long periods of convalescence.

Against this mélange of high finance, sophistication, fiery artistic temperaments, hard work, and uncertain health the Arctic became a refuge. But even more important, as James Houston pointed out, it catered to Gimpel's restlessness: "Charles liked variety, I think, a sane life sometimes with *civilized* friends – then – Bang! straight into a hard life with rough *primitive* friends."[14] In this sense Gimpel's rhythm of life during the 1950s and 1960s was not unlike that of many urbanized southern Canadians who, according to his friend the Canadian historian W.L. Morton, penetrated the wilderness and returned to "civilization" at regular intervals.[15]

Late nineteenth- and early twentieth-century adventurer-explorers were not the only people who were drawn to the Arctic and photographed it once they got there. For government-sponsored ethnologists, geological surveyors, cartographers, and scientists such as Robert Bell, Albert Peter Low, and Graham Drinkwater, photographs were part of the documenting and map-making process. They reinforced Canada's sovereignty over a vast territory; they promoted its natural resources; and they imposed southern Canada's economic, social, and legal hegemony over the Inuit men and women who lived there. Not surprisingly the photographs they took of the indigenous peoples were, in keeping with the wishes of the physical anthropologists, of the "mug shot" variety: head and shoulders, front and back, or full-face and profile.[16] All of these photographers looked for sameness not difference, types not individuals.[17] By so doing they put their Inuit subjects firmly into the sub-category of "the other."

The photographs that missionaries took of Inuit men and women during the early years of the twentieth century were no less impersonal. Convinced that "the true romance of the Arctic missionary" lay in helping the Inuit to "pass from a sinful and degraded paganism into the faith and practice of Jesus Christ," Archibald Lang Fleming, who opened the first Anglican mission at Lake Harbour (Kimmiruq) on Baffin Island in 1909, placed photographs of criminal-looking "heathen" Inuit alongside photographs of smiling Inuit who had been "saved."[18] Far from using photographs as a way of celebrating the closeness of the Inuit to the land, Fleming, along with many other apostles of Christ, employed the medium to condemn it.[19] Yet as the missionaries well knew, the ill-health and poverty of the Inuit was not due to their "savagery" but had come about largely as a result of their contact with non-indigenous peoples.

The incorporation of Inuit peoples of the Eastern Arctic into the social, economic, and political sphere of southern Canada began long before Britain handed over the North-west Territories to the Dominion in 1880. In the early part of the nineteenth century tuberculosis and other diseases were introduced by Scottish and American whalers. Incidents of starvation, which were not unknown among the Inuit, became more frequent during the latter part of the nineteenth century due to over-hunting, thanks to the availability of rifles, and, from the early 1950s, as a result of the Canadian government's re-location programmes. Thinking that the Inuit might enjoy a better standard of living if they returned to their "natural state" and wanting to ensure Canada's sovereignty over remote areas by populating it, the government moved several families to uninhabited areas of the Arctic. Lacking adequate food, unable to cope without the amenities offered by the trading post, most experienced severe hardships.

Compulsory education and dependent-making social services which had forced the Inuit to move from inland camps into the White-dominated coastal settlements where those services were available presented a very different problem. While Maata Pudlat of Cape Dorset (Kinngait) would have preferred to remain on the land where food was more plentiful, she "had no choice, because it was so hard for so many families to be apart from their children who were attending school."[20] The result was an acute feeling of dislocation among the Inuit peoples.

Nor was the disruption of their hunting economy of their own making. The Inuit participated in the whaling industry from the early nineteenth century, in fur-trapping from the early twentieth, and in craft-making from the mid-1950s. Involvement in these among other industries such as sealing put them at the mercy of market cycles, company policies, and trends in fashion. When the price of white fox pelts plummeted after the

Second World War, for example, those who had earned a living from trapping sought employment as construction workers at the newly established weather and radar stations, on the air strips, or in the mines and the craft centres. Seasonal and short-term, these jobs replaced one unstable form of employment with another.

The arrival of Roman Catholic and Anglican missionaries was equally threatening to their social and cultural traditions. At first the new Christian "taboos" were simply adapted to the old Inuit ones; then in some cases they replaced them altogether. "There was a change after a minister came from Pangnirtung to tell us about God," Atoat Akitirq of Arctic Bay remembered, and we had to "give up our evil ways."[21] Abe Okpik recalled his experience more dramatically: "They told us that we would burn in hell if we didn't follow their religion."

Yet the photographic image of the Inuit that southern Canadians saw in religious, government, and scientific publications, in popular magazines, and in Arctic memoirs and adventure stories up to the middle of the twentieth century was that of the anonymous, ever-smiling, childlike, and above all uncomplaining "Noble Savage." Only two photographers had dared to present the Inuit as anything else. One was an outsider – Robert Flaherty, the American-born prospector, mineralogist, Arctic explorer, photographer, and filmmaker. The other was an Inuk trapper and one-time employee of the Baffin Trading Company, Peter Pitseolak, who lived in Kiaktuk where he was camp boss over ten families, then in Cape Dorset on Baffin Island.

Taken between 1910 and 1921, Flaherty's photographs give a sensitive account of a people confronting the first stage of the Euro-Canadian invasion of the Eastern Arctic. Yet until the 1970s these photographs of Inuit staring into Flaherty's lens, remained unknown. What was known and popularized throughout most of the century was Flaherty's 1922 film, *Nanook of the North*. With a good deal of artistic licence, romanticising, and condescension Flaherty presented his hero as a "Nobel Victim." Nanook the hunter struggles to kill a walrus with a harpoon when rifles were the common weapon. He shivers in his snowhouse (*igluvigaq*) because Flaherty had to remove its top in order to shoot the film sequence. (Snowhouses are remarkably warm.) Nanook wears polar bear skin pants which were not worn by the Inummariit in Northern Quebec where the film was made. And finally, he seems oblivious to the amenities offered by the White settlement of Port Harrison (Inukjuak) where the Inuit had long been trading their fox pelts for tobacco, enamel mugs, kettles, tea, flour, and sugar. By thus presenting Nanook as a victim of the harsh and intractable Arctic climate, Flaherty rolled up all of the misguided clichés associated with the Inuit into the most fashionable medium of the day: the film. A sad indication of the extent to which myth can sometimes imitate real life came two years after *Nanook of the North* was released. Alakariallak, the Inummariit hunter from the Northern Ungava Peninsula, who portrayed Nanook in the film, died of starvation while on a hunting trip. In the end Alakariallak had become the "Noble Victim" he had so successfully portrayed in the film.

Peter Pitseolak's photographs were better known, at least among the Inuit. The highly respected photographer had acquired his first camera – a fixed-focus Brownie – from a Roman Catholic priest in the early 1940s. By the time he stopped taking pictures thirty years later, he had compiled a seminal record of his two Innuk wives, Annie then Aggeok, and their seven children, of the people who passed through Kiaktuk, of Cape Dorset where he lived in the 1940s and again from the 1960s until his death in 1973, and, finally, of the patients in the southern sanatorium where he spent the early part of the 1940s and the mid-1950s undergoing medical treatment, first for a kidney ailment, then for tuberculosis. Though Pitseolak offered an unromantic view in the candid photographs he took of his family, his friends, and of virtually everyone who passed through Kiaktuk and Cape Dorset over the course of three decades, he did not steer entirely clear of the nostalgia which had set Flaherty off course when he made *Nanook of the North*. Like Flaherty, whom he had met as a boy in 1913 or 1914, Pitseolak preferred to depict his people as they had lived in the past. Consequently he took care to photograph his family in traditional clothing. (One caribou parka [*amauti*] and sealskin pants went the rounds several times.) He instructed his friends to fish and set traps in the traditional way so that he could make a record of these fast-disappearing traditions. And he also had them act out the "well-known adventure of Taktillitak, a man who lived in the lifetime of Peter Pitseolak's father and whose exploits were legendary" so that he could photograph it for posterity.[22] Pitseolak did not photograph these things because he wished, like Flaherty, to present the Inuit as heroic survivors of a harsh climate, but because he wanted to show how his people had lived in harmony with it. As he told his daughter Kooyoo Ottochie, "in the future people were not going to wear any more caribou clothing." This made him want to "take pictures before it vanished so his grandchildren could see something of the old way."[23] As Innumarit, or the one who understands the true Inuit ways, Pitseolak was the right person to do it.

Gimpel was unwilling to sacrifice the present for the past by re-creating the earlier way of life of the Inuit in his photographs. Aware that societies are not static but in a constant state of transition, he photographed their new professions such as mining, radio broadcasting, house painting, Ski-Doo riding, and printmaking with as much care as he recorded their traditional forms of occupation.[24] He showed the extent to which the Inuit had become dependent on the material culture of the South. The side of a scavenged packing crate becomes the door of a skin tent (*tupiq*). One Inuk boy sports a holster, another hides behind a mask fashioned out of a package of Player's cigarettes. An otherwise traditionally clad Inuk man wears sun-glasses and Kingwatsiak and his daughter Anna live in a government-issued plastic styrofoam snowhouse.

Gimpel's fascination with the changing world of the Inuit did not make him neglect the White community who had been in and out of the Canadian Eastern Arctic since Martin Frobisher first sighted Baffin Island in 1576. Photographs of missionaries, the Royal Canadian Mounted Police, ship's captain and crew, along with Hudson's Bay Company personnel, schoolteachers, and anthropologists were taken with a great deal of humour and irony. Mocking Euro-Canadian officials in his sharp voice – Gimpel was always "abrasive in argument" and "rich in contradictions" – was a favourite pastime.[25] In fact Gimpel took great pleasure in starting an argument between a trader and a priest, or a schoolteacher and a mounted policeman. On one occasion he even risked freezing to death for the sake of making a good joke. Following James Houston's instructions that he meet a plane bringing important government officials from the South to Cape Dorset, "Charles came down, dressed in his red silk bathrobe and slippers." "His appearance," James Houston continued, "was extraordinary in a temperature of -35 C." However, it had the desired effect, because "the officials were speechless."[26]

It was not without a sense of irony, then, that Gimpel photographed a poker-faced Mrs. Beard sitting in her spick-and-span venetian-blinded, frilly-curtained 1950s kitchen. (It could have been anywhere in Canada but happened to be the Hudson's Bay Company staff house in the remote settlement of Lake Harbour only a few hundred kilometres below the Arctic Circle.) Or that he caught two Mounties standing in undignified poses at their headquarters in Frobisher Bay (Iqaluit). Or that a priest, dressed in elaborate robes and surrounded by the paraphernalia of his profession, was photographed as he was about to say mass in a four-berth cabin on the *M.V. Rupertsland*. Gimpel's ability to move with such ease between the Native and non-Native communities is not surprising: as James Houston put it Charles used to "go native" in his own city. From his South Kensington home in London he made frequent photographic expeditions to the less-privileged, though more colourful, areas of the city such as Brixton where he was known among its residents by another name. "If anyone asks for Charlie Gimple," James Houston was told while visiting Gimpel, "It's me."[27] The villagers in Ménerbes at his summer home in Provence also became subjects for his camera. Equally, the social division of village life in Cretingham had, according to the writer Ronald Blythe, "no reality for him." During his months of convalescence at Ivy Cottage, Gimpel "was able to understand and welcome the characteristics of his farm-worker and craftsmen neighbours in such a way that, for some years, he held a very special place in their hearts."[28]

Self-portrait, Charles Gimpel,
Cape Dorset, 1 April 1968

Gimpel's photographer contemporaries Gontran de Poncins and Richard Harrington, to name just two, moved with equal ease between the Native and non-Native communities in the Canadian Eastern Arctic. But unlike Gimpel, they placed the increasingly westernized Inuit squarely into the "Noble Savage" or "Noble Victim" stereotype. These late-romantic photographers of the 1940s and 1950s drew on an array of visual devices and iconographic clichés: action poses echoing Franz Boas's faked photographs; low-angled shots of silhouetted figures popularized by Flaherty in *Nanook of the North;* and closely cropped, full-faced portraits developed first in the late nineteenth century by Julia Margaret Cameron, then popularized during the inter-war years by photographers attached to the Farm Security Administration programme in the United States or who provided photographic copy for the *Saturday Evening Post.*[29]

The extent to which the combination of these visual devices had led to a romanticized view of the Inuit was demonstrated in 1950. In March of that year Richard Harrington, a Toronto-based photo-journalist, encountered a group of starving Padleimiut on the South Keewatin Plains west of the Hudson Bay. Conditioned to seeing photographs of the happy-go-lucky, hardy Inuit, the Canadian public were shocked when Harrington's photographs of the emaciated Padleimiut hit the front page of the *Toronto Daily Star.* (Forced to respond to the public outrage, an RCAF aircraft dropped sacks of dried peas and beans into the area. Lacking fuel to cook them, the Padleimiut continued to starve.) Harrington hoped that his pictures would "show the outside world what real suffering was."[30] But the devices he employed to accomplish this – he cropped the portraits and added captions[31] which assured the public that the starving Padleimiut were uncomplaining – not only served to obscure the horrific conditions in which they were living, but did nothing to explain how the situation had come about in the first place. The publication of Farley Mowat's provocative book, *People of the Deer,* two years later attempted to explain how eight Padleimiut had died of starvation within six months due to the Canadian government's *experimental* relocation schemes.[32] Like Nanook, the Padleimiut were thus transformed from "Noble Savages" into "Noble Victims."

Gimpel was never confronted with a situation of such horrific dimensions. Yet when he did encounter subjects that were clearly out of step with the stereotypical view, he made no attempt to avoid or to soften them. He showed the extent to which a tent, inhabited by an Inuit family living in Sugluk (Salluit), was in complete disarray. He took two remarkable series of photographs dealing with the controversial issue of fox trapping. One group records the suffocation of a white fox caught in a steel leg-hold trap on line; the other shows Qaqyuraqyuk skinning a fox, in one piece.

According to the geographer Terence Armstrong, Gimpel was aware that "he was doing things differently from other people" in his photographs.[33] His ability to create a powerful and authoritative image within the very limited range of tones offered by the black-and-white photograph, without falling back upon the clichés and devices of his predecessors and his contemporaries, was due to his strong, individualistic, and sometimes combative personality on the one hand, and his acute sense of humour and irony on the other. The combination of these traits nourished his understanding of, respect for, and acceptance by the Inuit peoples. His knowledge of contemporary art – particularly his appreciation of space – helped him to see the multitudinous dimensions of the Arctic landscape and the people in it. "He was not just trying to tell a story in his photographs," Kov Parr replied when asked why he felt Charles's photographs were different from those of other photographers, "but showing something that was just there."

IT WOULD BE a mistake to attempt to understand Charles Gimpel's photographs solely in terms of how they relate to those of other early and contemporary photographers, or how they are a product of Gimpel's own personality, knowledge, and experiences. The form, the venue, and the viewer all play a part in determining how they are seen. As Julian Bell recently wrote, photographs are not unlike viruses. They "get around the world attaching themselves unpredictably to new contexts, reproducing and mutating beyond any scheme and control, lacking any body they can truly call their own."[34] Shown over three decades, in a number of different venues and contexts, this is precisely what happened to Gimpel's photographs. As a backdrop for the Gimpel Fils' early exhibitions of Inuit sculpture and drawings they served to authenticate the art that was being produced by "primitive" men clad in parkas, sitting out of doors with chisel in hand, carving. Illustrated in the pages of the Hudson's Bay Company's magazine, *The Beaver,* Gimpel's photographs of westernized Inuit made the point that the Inuit transition from one culture to another had been successful. When a representative number were circulated by the Smithsonian Institution, on the heels of two exhibitions of Inuit art, they showed the extent to which the Inuit were caught between two cultures. Kept by Cape Dorset residents such as Kov Parr and Iyola Kingwatsiak, Gimpel's photographs provide images of long-departed family members and friends and awaken memories of Charles himself. And shown in 1992 at a Cambridge graduate college, they were viewed in wonder by visiting fellows from around the world, many of whom saw them as proof that the Inuit, who are about to become masters once again of their own land, had indeed survived the Euro-Canadian invasion.

GIMPEL'S PHOTOGRAPHS can thus be read on many levels. We can view them as one photographer's changing vision of a land and its people. They enable us to observe how the Inuit responded to Gimpel differently as they got to know him better. And, just as significantly, we can consider their value as historical and social-anthropological records: they document the Inuit response to the westernization and the modernization of their material culture in terms of clothing, modes of transportation, and house building, among other things, over a crucial ten-year period.

Whatever these photographs are, they are not inert. Their making involved a kind of collusion between the photographer and the subject. Their interpretation continues another sort of complicity, this time between the presenter and the viewer. We may therefore enjoy Gimpel's photographs as aesthetic objects, view them as historical records, or consider them in relation to the work of other photographers. However we choose to look at them, we must not forget that they represent the changing vision of one man whose perspective partook of different roles: that of the Arctic tourist, that of the archaeologist, that of the ethnologist, that of the art dealer, and that of the photographer. And, not least of all, they provide the Inuit of Cape Dorset who possess his photographs with a visual record of their families and friends.

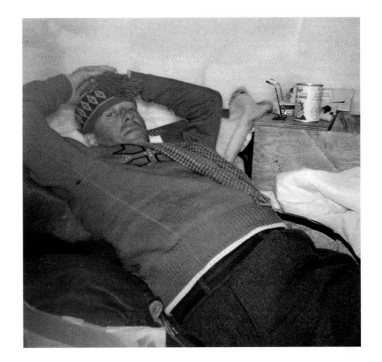

Self-portrait, Charles Gimpel in snowhouse, April 1964

'I GO RAMBLING
WITH MY CAMERA'

I count it an unexpected stroke of good fortune, the day the Hudson's Bay Company commissioned me

as an amateur to do a photographic survey of some of their most northern posts in the Eastern arctic.

I was their guest for six weeks on board the supply ship, M.V. Rupertsland. *It so happened that I*

knew something about the Eskimo way of life and I already appreciated their remarkable gift for

making small stone carvings. By the end of that trip covering several thousand miles, I had not only

increased my knowledge but had developed a passion for the arctic.[1]

Charles Gimpel, 1961

CHARLES GIMPEL WAS no ordinary tourist when he boarded the *M.V. Rupertsland* at Churchill, Manitoba, in late August of 1958. Having mounted an exhibition of Inuit art at his London gallery in 1953, he was the first European art dealer to recognize the artistic qualities of Inuit sculpture. A collector of books dealing with all aspects of the Arctic, Gimpel's library embraced the journals and recollections of early explorers, Inuit ethnographies, the official reports of government-sponsored expeditions, the dynamic illustrations of adventurer-photographers, as well as books by such controversial authors as Farley Mowat.[2] Gimpel was, therefore, well prepared to cast his Arctic experience into whatever context he chose: historical, visual, mythical, or critical. Moreover, his mandate to record "some of the most northern points in the Eastern Arctic" for *The Beaver* magazine gave him a special status among his fellow passengers. (The ship's company included schoolteachers, physicians, carpenters, a priest, Hudson's Bay Company personnel, a few tourists, and a crew headed by a soft-spoken, blue-eyed, and rather sad-looking Welshman by the name of Captain A.C. Lloyd.)

Travelling through the region in the late Arctic summer, Gimpel saw no snowhouse (*igluvigaq*), ice-locked settlement, or sleds (*qamutiik*) drawn by dogteams (*qimuksiit*) of up to fifteen huskies a piece. And confined to a ship with stops just long enough to unload the mail bags, the oil drums, the foodstuffs, and the other supplies that would sustain the community throughout the winter and spring, there was no opportunity to visit the outpost camps lying within one or two days' journey of every permanent settlement. Yet "Big Ship Time" (*Umiakjuakkanak*), as it had been called ever since the European and American whalers visited the small Eastern Arctic communities in the nineteenth century, had its own attractions. It was a festive occasion. The ship's tourists swaddled their heads in mosquito netting and explored the area surrounding the settlement. And the few residents of the non-Native community rowed or paddled from the shore to the ship in search of gossip and news from the crew.

"Big Ship Time" not only brought news and much-needed supplies to every

Previous page: Nashuk and Iqqluk sitting on the beach at Igloolik, 13 September 1958

permanent settlement, it brought employment. "When the ship arrived," Peter Pitseolak of Cape Dorset recalled, "we went on and worked for two or three days."[3] Some, like Kupa Tayara of Sugluk, served as pilots on the boat, though most, like Taitusie from Igloolik (Iglulik), waded into the water and carried provisions on their backs from the scows to the shore. Still others just sat on the beach and watched. Although uneventful compared with the trips that Charles subsequently made in the Arctic, his first was exotic enough to make him want to return.

THE MANITOBA SETTLEMENT where the *M.V. Rupertsland* began its voyage to the High Arctic had been a military stronghold for the British during the early part of the eighteenth century. All that was left of the fur-trading empire when Charles arrived there in 1958 were the crumbling stone bastions of Fort Prince of Wales. The port's two-and-a-half-million-bushel grain elevator, located across the harbour from the fort, now dominated the town.[4] From Churchill the *M.V. Rupertsland* sailed up the west coast of Hudson Bay to the mouth of Rankin Inlet (Kangiraniq). After spending a day anchored five miles off the coast while waiting for the weather to clear, the ship entered the inlet. It was the fifth of September. Gimpel scrambled around the North Rankin Nickel Mine which had drawn the bulk of its labour force – some 107 workers – from the Inuit who lived in Chesterfield Inlet (Igluliqaarjuk) and Eskimo Point (Arviat). (Providing workers for the mine was one goal of the federal government's relocation programme mentioned earlier.) He also visited a settlement comprising some thirty newly constructed three-room pre-fabricated houses which had been built half a mile from the mine for the Inuit workers and their families. And, as would become his habit in every port of call, he photographed the children.

The two-and-a-half-million-bushel grain

elevator in Churchill, Manitoba,

30 August 1958

Children playing in the schoolyard during

their recess at Chesterfield Inlet,

5 September 1958

After leaving Rankin the ship sailed further up the Hudson Bay coast to Chesterfield Inlet. It was here that Charles encountered something that he found "terrible": the Joseph Bernier Federal School and the Turquetil Hall student residence. "Nearly all of the kids come from all over the North, some hundreds of miles away," he wrote of the Roman Catholic residence and federal school at Chesterfield Inlet, and "are brought in by planes and stay 9 months at boarding school." He spent a day photographing the children playing in the school yard, during recess, attending their first classes of the school year, sipping a mug of hot chocolate while sitting in the school corridor "back against wall and legs stretched out Eskimo fashion," eating their evening meal of raw meat and frozen fish at long gender-segregated tables, and, under the strict eye of the Grey Nuns of Montreal and Nicolet, preparing for bed in dormitories of fifty cots to a room.[5]

On the 6th day of September the weather broke as the ship left Hudson Bay. Dressed only in his shirt sleeves, Charles photographed the slowly moving pans of sea ice and the coastal landscape beyond in order to show "how lovely it can be in the Arctic."[6] Two days later the ship dropped anchor in Sugluk, a small Inuit settlement on the northern shore of the Ungava Peninsula. There Gimpel purchased his first work of art on the voyage, a carving by Tivi from nearby Ivujivik, for which he paid the Northern Service Officer, Mr. Fluck, twenty-five dollars. He met the colourful Oblate Priest Father Verspeeck, a Belgian who sported a beautiful long-flowing beard, displayed a passion for dogs and his shortwave radio. He then encountered the less-colourful Anglican minister Mr. Elles. Later, at the Hudson's Bay Company staff house he discovered "quite a different type of Post Manager."[7] Tall, thin, and young, Mr. Tetters played the violin, possessed a good collection of books and gramophone records, and wore his school tie.

The Inuit settlement, comprising a dozen oblong tents erected eight hundred yards from the shore, was split down the middle by the complex of T-shaped wooden buildings inhabited by the non-Native community. Charles visited and photographed the interiors of two tents. "The mess is quite unbelievable," he wrote of his first encounter with how the

displaced Inuit lived, "with everything strewn on the floor: clothing, food, cooking utensils, primus stoves, carcasses, duffels, old skins, piles of packing cases."[8] After bidding
farewell to the British schoolteacher Monica Hember, who was in tears because her lug-
gage could not be found when she disembarked and she had no chance of replacing it for
another year, the *M.V. Rupertsland* crossed Hudson Strait.

The following morning the ship reached the south coast of the Foxe Peninsula on
Baffin Island and, under an overcast sky, dropped anchor off Dorset Island. Large pans
of sea ice still dotted the bay or were banked along the shore. Cape Dorset had been ice
bound for longer than usual that summer. An effort to restock the settlement in July had
almost ended in disaster when the crew of an amphibian relief aircraft were stranded for
thirty-three days on the bay ice which had been blown out to sea. By mid-morning the
weather had cleared and a flotilla consisting of Peterhead boats, kayaks, and canoes made
its way to the ship. Among the passengers was "a young, tough, good looking man" who
upon meeting Charles said, "not Gimpel Fils?"[9] Thus began Charles's friendship with James
Houston, the Northern Service Officer, artist, and arts adviser who had done more in the
recent past than any other non-Native to promote Inuit art. Along with Houston, Gimpel
met the Hudson's Bay Company post manager Bill Hall and his wife, Helen, who insisted
on telling him that she loved the North and could "not visualize living outside."[10]

Two days later the *M.V. Rupertsland* sailed around the Foxe Peninsula on Baffin
Island, headed north through the open patches of water off the Foxe Basin, crossed the
Arctic Circle, and reached the most northern point of its journey, Igloolik, located on an
island off the north-east coast of Melville Peninsula. An abundance of pack ice had prevented both the Hudson's Bay Company's supply ship and the Canadian government's Eastern
Arctic Patrol vessel from restocking the small settlement the previous year. When the *M.V.
Rupertsland* arrived, the Oblate Fathers Danielo and Francis eagerly fell upon the mail bags;
the Hudson's Bay Company post manager happily supervised the unloading of supplies into
the Company's white, green-trimmed warehouse built well above the shore. After Gimpel

had negotiated the purchase of four more carvings and taken photographs of the men and women unloading the ship, or just sitting on the beach, the *M.V. Rupertsland* turned southward and retraced its journey.

The ship stopped in Cape Dorset long enough to allow Charles to photograph Father Trinel settling into his home, Tunu carving a seal oil lamp (*qulliq*), and eight members of the Pee family squeezed into their tent. There were two more stops, at Lake Harbour (Kimmiruq) and Frobisher Bay, before the ship headed north again. This time the *M.V. Rupertsland* sailed up the east coast of Baffin Island. Its destination, Pangnirtung, was a small settlement straddling the southeastern shore of Pangnirtung Fjord on the north shore of Cumberland Sound. This was the last Inuit community in the Arctic that Charles would visit before heading south to Montreal. Surrounded by steep mountain walls, their height exaggerated by a sprinkling of early snow, Pangnirtung was a magnificent last port of call.

On his five-and-a-half-thousand-kilometre journey, during which "his film expenditure ran into the thousands of feet,"[11] Gimpel responded to what he saw and experienced with a naïveté that was both charming and predictable. To help himself understand what was new, he compared it with what was known to him. During the three-day train journey from Winnipeg to Churchill, for example, he noted in his journal that every *village* had a grain elevator and that the *square* in front of the station at The Pas was riddled with potholes.[12] He compared the width of the streets in Churchill to that of the *Avenue des Champs Elysées* in Paris; its quality of the light to the famous Cornish art colony of St. Ives in the south of England. And he found that the landscape surrounding Sugluk Inlet was comparable in beauty to the more remote areas of Ireland and Scotland. Even the residence and school at Chesterfield Inlet, whose attendance, according to the testimony of one former pupil was a very painful experience,[13] possessed, in Gimpel's words, an "*air de fête*" because one enter-prising priest broadcast light opera arias throughout the settlement during the evenings.

When Gimpel was unable to comprehend the new by comparing it with the famil-iar, he fell back upon cliché, used his imagination, or drew upon what he had read. After the train pulled out of The Pas, which lay amidst flat scrub growth halfway between Win-nipeg and Churchill, he noted that it was crowded with "bushmen and miners" dressed in "loud cheque [sic] shirts" and sporting "weather beaten faces which suggests their open air living habits."[14] When he encountered the foul smell around the tents at Sugluk, it must, he thought, be "the stench I have read about" resulting from "the decaying meat which was given to the huskies."[15] And when he met a group of Chippewyan Indians at the Hudson's Bay Company store in Churchill he mistakenly assumed them to be Inuit. Gimpel's imagi-nation, along with his reading and his comparative references, were sometimes insufficient in helping him understand what was new. When this happened he recorded what he saw and experienced in meticulous detail. After descending a three-hundred-foot shaft to the lowest level of the North Rankin Nickel Mine, for example, he vividly described how he and the mine captain, Paul Prou of Montreal, crawled "on our tummies through tunnels which are barely big enough," climbed "up steep mud like slopes with a hundred and fifty foot drop in darkness," scaled "ladders which have been put up vertically into narrow fun-nels," and encountered "strange and beautiful stagmytes [sic] growing like mushrooms and rare flowers from the ground."[16]

While putting his experiences into words helped him bridge the gap between ignorance and comprehension, Gimpel was not content to be a mere observer. From the moment he bought his checked shirts and long-john flannel underwear at the Hudson's Bay Company store in Winnipeg, he wanted not only to fit in but to participate. In a Churchill beer parlour he quickly caught on to the local custom of ordering two beers at a time. In Sugluk he made a serious effort "to get used to" the stench even though the rotting meat "nearly made . . . [him] puke."[17] And wherever he was, Gimpel asked everyone he met about "the Eskimo Problem."[18]

Gimpel soon discovered, however, that "the Eskimo question . . . [was] a very touchy one" because "few people . . . [were] prepared to stick their neck out" and discuss it.[19] Nevertheless over a beer – two beers – in Churchill with George Lush, the legendary fur trapper-cum-night watchman, and Bill Carson of the Hudson's Bay Company he was told that there was "no reason why Eskimos should starve." When he asked how the Inuit could be prevented from so doing, both men were "a bit vague about a constructive policy."[20] On board the *M. V. Rupertsland* he gathered further opinions regarding the Inuit from his fellow passengers. Peter Nichols, the Hudson's Bay Company manager of the Arctic division, who "showed infinite patience in answering . . . [Gimpel's] endless questions on the North" throughout the voyage, told Charles that southern Canadians were "going too fast" in forcing their way of life on the Inuit.[21] Father Trinel, who had been in the Garry Lake region just before eighteen Inuit in that community had died of starvation, berated the government for doing nothing to avert the disaster. And two British schoolteachers who had just taken a month-long course in Ottawa on how to teach the Inuit felt that the solution to "the Eskimo Problem" lay in teaching them self-preservation. Though he found Monica Hember and Betty Adams "a bit drunk with a missionary and frontier spirit," theirs was an attitude that struck a sympathetic chord with Gimpel.[22]

Almost everyone blamed the government for "the Eskimo Problem." Gordon Robertson's Department of Northern Affairs and Natural Resources which had taken full responsibility for the welfare of the Inuit peoples since its creation in 1953 and Prime Minister John Diefenbaker whose "northern vision" focused on northern resources rather than on the northern peoples both came into the firing line. Determined to help make the Inuit self-reliant, to open up the North's economic resources, and to maintain Canada's sovereignty in the High Arctic at the same time, the government despatched nurses and welfare workers, teachers like Monica Hember, doctors and Northern Service Officers like James Houston to the North. This new breed of workers from southern Canada threatened to displace the triumvirate composed of RCMP officers, missionaries, and Hudson's Bay

Company post managers who had long fostered varying degrees of social, cultural, spiritual, and economic dependency among the Inuit. Frustrated by the shift in government policy and by their own inability to help prevent the Inuit from starving or from filling southern Canadian hospitals with almost twenty per cent of their population, the old triumvirate found a scapegoat in the new breed of government-sponsored workers who they claimed had volunteered to work in the North for the wrong reasons. Seeking "a quicker way to promotion," "making money," and, attempting to solve "their own problems in the frozen north" were some of the accusations which Gimpel carefully noted in his journal.[23]

The Euro-Canadian community had to find a way of educating the Inuit "up to University standards so as to be able to make [them into] doctors and top administrators, lawyers, teachers etc." Self-determination would, Gimpel felt, put an end to the conflicting signals that the Inuit were getting from various quarters of the White community. It would also help eradicate what he observed as "the growing segregation which is already appearing in the Arctic."[24] The extent to which this was true was certainly evident in Gimpel's photographs: the homes of the Euro-Canadians tower above the much smaller Inuit tents, Butler buildings, and matchbox houses. And the spacious "Whites only" dining-room at the North Rankin Nickel Mine dominates the small, crowded Inuit canteen next to it.

THREE MONTHS AFTER Gimpel had returned to London, his film passed through the experienced hands of his printer Miss Deste. He declared mixed results: "some of them are good, others disappointing."[25] Yet as he told Frank Walker, the Hudson's Bay Company official who had commissioned him to make a record of the company's outposts in the Eastern Arctic, "I was thrilled with my trip." And, he added, "I can only hope that my photographs will please the Hudson's Bay Company and will justify the commission."[26]

They did. Southern Canadians who saw the spring issue of *The Beaver* in 1959 were presented with a selection of Gimpel's photographs, which centred around his Arctic adventure, in an article titled "Ports of Call."[27] Carefully chosen, they fit nicely into the Company's public relations strategy of transmitting a view of the Inuit as healthy and happy people.[28] After the article had appeared, a selection of Gimpel's Arctic photographs were exhibited at the Gimpel Fils as a backdrop for the Inuit carvings he had collected on his trip. The response to both the carvings and the photographs was so favourable that Charles was more determined than ever to return to the Arctic.[29] But as Franz Boas had discovered more than fifty years earlier, getting back to the Arctic was no easy matter. Gimpel's appeal to the Hudson's Bay Company to send him to the Western Arctic the following year came to nothing. His letters to James Houston went unanswered. Since there were no commercial flights between most northern communities, no hotels, restaurants, or any of the other amenities that a traveller to the Arctic might find today, Gimpel needed the assistance of a Hudson's Bay Company post manager, a Northern Service Officer, or a government agent of some kind.

It would be more than three years before Gimpel would return to the Arctic and go, as he put it, "rambling with my camera."[30]

Three Inuit miners working at the 300-foot
level of the North Rankin Nickel Mine,
4 September 1958

The headmistress in a classroom at the
Joseph Bernier Federal School,
Chesterfield Inlet, 5 September 1958

A classroom at the Joseph Bernier Federal

School in Chesterfield Inlet,

5 September 1958

Girls in the dining-hall at Turquetil Hall
Residence, Chesterfield Inlet,
5 September 1958

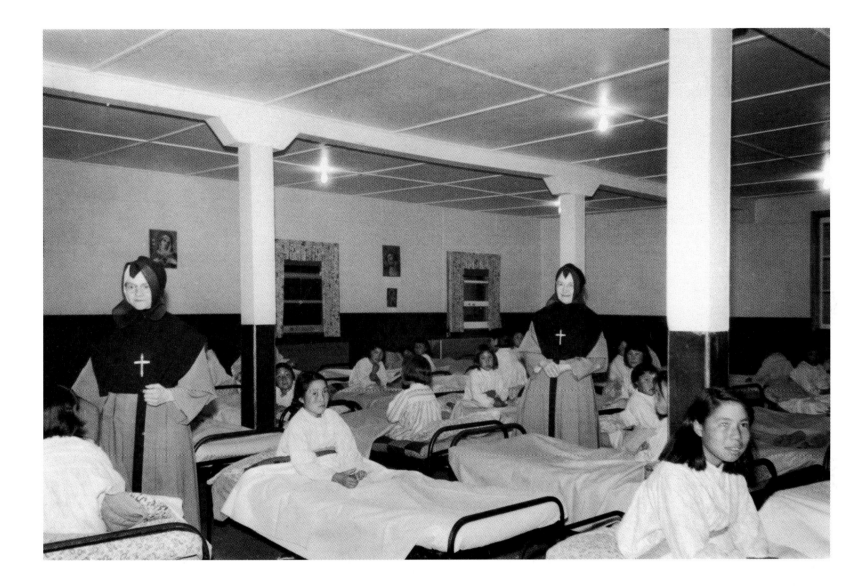

Girls in the Turquetil Hall Residence

before bedtime, Chesterfield Inlet,

5 September 1958

Tent at Sugluk. Note the skins being dried,

8 September 1958

Inuk child holding harpoon near the shore,

Sugluk, 8 September 1958

Monica Hember, the British schoolteacher,

just before disembarking at Sugluk,

8 September 1958

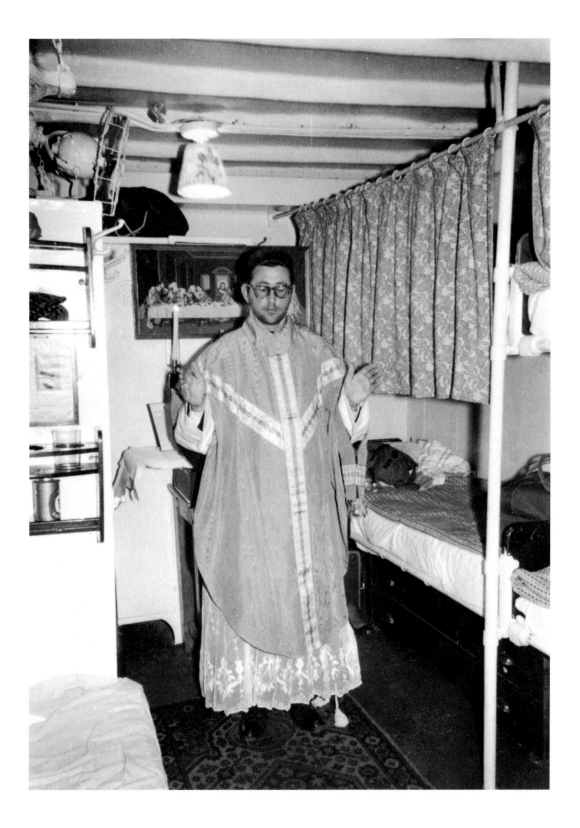

Father Trinel giving mass in his cabin on
the *M.V. Rupertsland*, 7 August 1958

Oblate Priest Father Verspeeck with
his radio equipment, Sugluk,
8 September 1958

Interior of an Inuit tent at Sugluk,

8 September 1958

Kupa Tayara piloting the *M.V. Rupertsland* through the icefields
lying between Sugluk and Cape Dorset, 9 September 1958

Peter Pitseolak unloading his boat at

Cape Dorset, 9 September 1958

Inuit men unloading drums of oil at

Cape Dorset, 9 September 1958

Five boys on the shore ice at Cape Dorset.
From left to right: Siala, Isohangitok, Etulu,
Aningmiuq, and Epiiruk, 9 September 1958

James Houston standing beside one of the prefabricated styrofoam

snowhouses sent to Cape Dorset by the Canadian government

in the mid-1950s, 9 September 1958

An Inuit family at "Big Ship Time" in
Cape Dorset, 16 September 1958

Father Trinel in his house at

Cape Dorset, 16 September 1958

The Pee family inside their tent at Cape Dorset.

From left to right: Nurluapik, Sau, Kumarjuk, Aoudla, Asiva, Sharnee,

Kakulu, and Itigajarjuaq, 16 September 1958

Tunu carving a seal oil lamp in Cape Dorset,

17 September 1958

Inuit graves at Igloolik,

12 September 1958

Evaluarjuk with her two children during
"Big Ship Time" at Igloolik,
12 September 1958

Oil drums lining the path to the Hudson's Bay

Company warehouse at Igloolik,

13 September 1958

Fathers Danielo and Francis opening mail
bags – the first delivery in two years – at Igloolik,
12 September 1958

Taitusie loading a bag of flour on to the back
of an Inuk woman at Igloolik,
13 September 1958

The icefields between Igloolik and Cape Dorset,

15 September 1958

Hudson's Bay Company buildings and Inuit tents

at Lake Harbour, 19 September 1958

Mrs. Beard with her child in the Hudson's Bay

Company staff house at Lake Harbour,

18 September 1958

Inuit carpenter building a Peterhead boat for
the Hudson's Bay Company at Lake Harbour,
19 September 1958

Inuit children helping to unload a scow at
Lake Harbour, 19 September 1958

Inuit men carrying a refrigerator up the bank

at Lake Harbour, 19 September 1958

Young Inuk boy wearing a holster at
Lake Harbour, 19 September 1958

Hudson's Bay Company boat-house at
Lake Harbour, 19 September 1958

Unloading during "Big Ship Time" at
Frobisher Bay, 23 September 1958

Preparing to unload the *M.V. Rupertsland* at

Pangnirtung, 26 September 1958

View of Pangnirtung from the
M.V. Rupertsland, 26 September 1958

Peter Nichols supervising the unloading

of a scow at Pangnirtung,

29 September 1958

Women in Pangnirtung stretching

a sealskin, 27 September 1958

Elessapee Ishulutaq (far left) and friends at

Pangnirtung, 27 September 1958

Solomon Kilabuk and Joanasie Simayuk
playing on the shore rocks
at Pangnirtung, 27 September 1958

Husky in front of a tent at Pangnirtung.

Note door made from a packing case,

30 September 1958

PART II

ART MADE FOR STRANGERS

My affection for the Eskimo, my interest in his economy, my travels to the Arctic are all well known

to my friends and to the art world. This might lead some to imagine that I bring to the study of the

carvings and the stone cuts a most uncritical and prejudiced eye.

However, this is by no means the case. My training as a dealer and a collector obliges me to

be as discerning, as demanding in this field of art as in any other. I know only too well that much

which comes out of the Arctic is very poor indeed. But the percentage of good work is similar, if

not higher, than in New York, London, and Paris. . . .[1]

Charles Gimpel, 1967

WHEN CHARLES GIMPEL wrote these lines in the autumn of 1967, southern Canadian enthusiasm for what has been called "art made for strangers" was at its height.[2] Whatever the occasion – birthday, anniversary or centennial celebration – a stone carving of a stalking bear, a supine seal, or an Inuk hunter was the most prestigious gift one could receive. These contemporary artefacts linked southern Canadians to their resource-rich hinterland and to their expansive yet little-explored northern frontier. They served as a counterpoint to the frequently inaccessible and sometimes meaningless canvases and sculptures produced by the followers of abstract expressionist art. They were evidence of the Canadian government's liberal-minded policy towards the country's indigenous peoples. But above all they were a talisman reminding urbanized Canadians that they were a northern people and therefore different from their neighbours to the south.

There can be no doubt that Charles Gimpel played a significant role in promoting "art made for strangers." By organizing exhibitions of Inuit art in Britain and in Europe he introduced this new art form to the European public. By treating Inuit sculpture as works of art he helped shift it from the museum to the art gallery. (The extent to which he believed Inuit sculpture to be art not artefact was made clear when in 1968 he unsuccessfully urged the Canadian government to make Inuit carvings part of their entry to the Venice Biennale.[3]) Finally, as some commentators have suggested, Gimpel may very well have prompted the Canadian government to become more fully involved in the production of Inuit art through his seminal Coronation exhibition in London in 1953.[4] Yet the origins of what some observers have mistakenly called the revival or renaissance of Inuit art did not begin with Gimpel or even with James Houston, the man whose name has been most closely associated with Inuit art since the end of the Second World War.[5] It began much earlier, with the Inuit themselves.

Carving skills had been long maintained by the Inuit not only through the production of tools but through the building of snowhouses. An artistic eye was required in order to cut each block of snow at right angles so that it would remain in place.[6] Skills such as

Previous page: Eeqeevudluk engraving a stone at the West Baffin Eskimo Co-operative in Cape Dorset, 3 May 1962

this were easily adapted to the production of curios and souvenirs when Scottish whalers first made their appearance in the early nineteenth century in the Eastern Arctic. Tobacco, metal objects, tea, and cloth were exchanged for country foods, fur clothing, navigational know-how, whaling skills, and curios. This activity continued into this century when RCMP officers, missionaries, adventurers, and traders, then teachers, government officials, construction workers, tourists, and other visitors from the South commissioned, bought, and traded carvings of model kayaks, sleds, animals, ashtrays, and even cribbage boards fashioned out of wood, ivory, bone, and to a lesser extent out of stone.

The production of these souvenir arts and crafts had little connection, according to the anthropologist Nelson Graburn, with "traditional Eskimo manufactures such as amulets, grave goods or decorated utensils, most of which had fallen out of use during the period of acculturation."[7] They were made for the trade, and, like fox pelts and sealskins, they complemented the diversified economy of the Inuit which blended subsistence with trade. But the extent to which the Inuit were producing souvenirs up to the middle of the twentieth century should not be exaggerated. It was hardly a full-time activity. As the celebrated artist Kenojuak told her biographer, Jean Blodgett: "In times of need, and when hunting was poor, we carved."[8]

THE CANADIAN GOVERNMENT recognized the economic possibilities of what they called "Eskimo handicrafts" as early as 1927. And even before that the Department of the Interior had collected native work "fearing that an increase in demands for curios and souvenirs, coupled with a changing material culture would soon lead to the disappearance of native articles."[9] But the government did little to encourage the actual production of Inuit crafts until it became clear, after the Second World War, that new forms of employment due to the decline in the price for furs, among other things, were essential. Thus in 1949 the

Northwest Territories Council awarded the Canadian Handicraft Guild, a private institution long committed to the making of indigenous handicrafts, a grant of $8,000.[10] With it the Guild commissioned the Toronto artist James Houston to purchase Native crafts from Eastern and Central Canadian Arctic settlements. Houston, who had visited Port Harrison in Northern Quebec on a painting expedition the previous year, was aware of the artistic and economic potential of Inuit crafts. Yet he felt that the emerging Inuit artist needed guidance if she or he was to produce work for the southern Canadian market. For this purpose he produced the carving manual, *Eskimo Handicrafts,* whose simple line drawings and accompanying syllabic text told future Inuit artists what sort of carvings would be "useful and acceptable to the white man."[11] The carvings Houston brought back from the Eastern Arctic during the next few years found enthusiastic buyers at the Canadian Handicraft Guild's annual sale in Montreal.

Within four years Houston had left the Guild and was working for the Department of Northern Affairs and National Resources. Initially he was based in Ottawa with the Arts and Crafts Section of the Department. Then, in 1956, Houston convinced the Department that he would be better able to "encourage a new and exciting field of Canadian art" if he were located in Cape Dorset.[12]

From the moment he arrived in Cape Dorset as Northern Service Officer in the summer of 1956 until he left in the autumn of 1961, Houston and his wife, Alma, capitalized on that settlement's "splendid carvers and sewers" in several ways.[13] Houston showed the Inuit how they could transform the bold and incisive drawings they had long made on stone, bone, and ivory into a variety of print mediums.[14] He found markets for their work both in and outside of the country. After setting up the Eskimo Craft Centre in Cape Dorset in 1958, he helped the Inuit establish their own co-operative, the West Baffin Eskimo Co-operative, a year later. From 1961 he gave advice to the "Eskimo Art Committee" (in 1967 it became the Canadian Arts Council) whose panel of non-Native museum and gallery officials from southern Canada passed "judgment on the quality of Eskimo art work submitted to their inspection."[15] He co-operated with art wholesaling agencies such as Canadian Arctic Producers, the Fédération des coopératives du nouveau Québec, the Hudson's Bay Company, and the first organization in the United States to handle Inuit art, Eskimo Art Incorporated. And, finally, Houston took every opportunity to publicize Inuit art by writing and by talking about it during his frequent lecture tours.[16]

In a number of government and commercial publications Houston extolled Inuit art as "primitive," "emotionally stimulating," and "intellectually rewarding."[17] He commended it for being "personal, created for the artist's satisfaction, not just for commercial ends." Made far from the centres of Western art, Houston was able to suggest that the "link between the past and the present. . .[was] as yet unbroken."[18] These views were in keeping with the romantic idea, popular during the 1950s and 1960s, that the so-called "primitive art of non-western societies" was superior to the self-conscious, frequently meaningless, and sophisticated art forms one found in more "advanced" societies.[19] Pure, intuitive, and vulnerable to extinction, Inuit art possessed both a sense of urgency and an otherness which enabled Houston to make it attractive to art investors and to a wide public.

Iyola Kingwatsiak preparing the
stone for a print at the Eskimo
Craft Centre, 17 May 1962

Quppapik carving in front of his home
at Cape Dorset, 30 April 1962

By the time Gimpel made his second trip to Cape Dorset in the spring of 1961, the infrastructure for the production, marketing, control, and mythologizing of Inuit art was in place. But observers often forget that what Houston and others like the schoolteacher Marjorie Hinds, the RCMP officer Constable R.D. Van Norman, the missionary Father Henri Tardy, and Hudson's Bay Company personnel Jim Bell and Peter Murdoch did to promote Inuit art was only half the story. Their schemes and programmes were a success because the Inuit were masters at meeting the demands of a foreign market.

"When we first started to carve," Bob Barnabas of Arctic Bay recalled, "we were sometimes told what to make, or that certain types of carvings were not wanted."[20] Upon learning "that abstract carvings were a waste of money as they didn't represent an animal and no one could tell what they were," Paniluk Qamanirq went back to carving animals.[21] And Arctic Bay carver David Ippirq discovered what his clientele in the South wanted by studying the examples of carvings illustrated in George Swinton's *Sculpture of the Eskimo* which appeared in 1962.[22] In this sense the Inuit were only one step removed from the Japanese "artists" who had long been realizing handsome profits from the sale of miniature carvings of totem poles to non-Native Canadians.

Whether they were carving, drawing, sewing, or printmaking, Inuit men and women quickly caught on to the tricks of the White trade. They learned that larger carvings sold better than smaller ones and that those with a pedestal and a favoured viewpoint were preferred to those carved in the round. They discovered that the work of some artists fetched higher prices than that of others – this prompted Kenojuak to sign drawings that had in fact been done by her husband, Johnniebo.[23] They quickly saw that the most highly sought after motifs were, in order of preference, "people, walrus, bears, seals, caribou, birds, fish [and] otter."[24] Finally, aware that southerners wanted time-conscious carvings, Inuit artists depicted actual events. In a society that prized group over individual effort, that did not produce art objects as such – there is no word in Inuktitut for art or artist – that possessed a static concept of time and space, and that had no art critics, ateliers, studios, salons, cafés, galleries, or any of the paraphernalia we associate with the production of art in the South, their achievement was monumental.

By 1967 seventy per cent of the people living in Cape Dorset earned more than half their annual income from craft-making. This did not come without considerable effort. "Making art for strangers" competed with other forms of employment such as hunting and trapping. "On good hunting days," James Houston recalled, "the printmakers simply disappeared but during the bad months and stormy periods they accomplished a prodigious amount of work."[25] "They think nothing," Houston wrote elsewhere, "of working from 8 in the morning until midnight on their job and usually have to be driven away from it at that hour."[26] Certainly Oshuitok Ipeelee remembered working in the Cape Dorset print shop "all day and night to improve the production in printing and to keep on going and it was quite tiring at times."[27] Producing for non-Native dealers, promoters, audiences, and curators had its problems too. George Akikuluk, a carver from Baffin Island's most northern settlement, Arctic Bay, felt that Inuit art was being used "to make a lot of profit for a lot of people" in the South. He was also concerned that southern Canadians, who possessed a limited knowledge of his culture, would fail to understand Inuit art when it was put on exhibition. In order to remedy this Akikuluk suggested that "the carvings could be accompanied by stories or explanations."[28]

The positive features of the art programme generally outweighed the negative ones, especially if one happened to live in Cape Dorset, which by 1972 had become known somewhat ambitiously, as the "Florence of the North."[29] By the end of the 1970s the commercial development of Inuit art had become a multi-million dollar enterprise.[30] But the success of the Inuit art programme could not only be measured in financial terms. "After Sowmik [James Houston's Inuit name meaning left-handed one] came there were many changes," Peter Pitseolak recalled in the early 1970s. "You could very easily notice that people started being their own bosses. They didn't listen any more to what was the right or wrong thing to do. They followed their own ideas."[31] George Swinton, the distinguished scholar of Inuit art, had already noted that "with the intrusion of Western ideas, there . . . [emerged] a decidedly ethnic consciousness, or, almost, an Eskimo nationalism, with a corresponding ethnic self-affirmation."[32] And Toronto art dealer Av Isaacs felt that the art industry was contributing not only to Inuit independence, but allowing "the Eskimo to buy time . . . [and thus] slow down their possible assimilation."[33]

But were the Inuit doing more than "buying time" and supplementing their shaky incomes by making prints, carvings, and drawings? James Houston and other promoters liked to think that the carving and printmaking process linked Inuit artists to their pre-contact magico-religious beliefs. Yet Paulosie Karvdluak claimed that she did not carve to produce "make-belief things." "What we show in our carvings," she continued, "is the life we have lived."[34] Representing the past, however, was not the purpose of every Inuit artist. Kenojuak's primary interest, according to Jean Blodgett, was with "the overall appearance of the image."[35]

Most southern observers avoided considering what the process of art-making meant for the Inuit. They chose to hold the carving or print at arm's length, and judge it according to contemporary Western art standards or to the work's indigenous roots. Thus Charles Martijn pronounced Inuit art as "a valid art form in its own right, and one of considerable merit" but nevertheless "of directed acculturation."[36] Another American anthropologist, the provocative Edmund Carpenter, dismissed the new art form altogether: "Its roots are Western: so is its audience." And, he continued, "their art should not be confused with aboriginal Eskimo art, which is of an entirely different order."[37]

Whether artefact, curio, souvenir, or work of art, whether linked to traditional or Western styles, motifs, and mediums, and whether representative of the Inuit past or present or merely an exercise in form and colour, the art enterprise did provide jobs, supplement incomes, boost confidence, help incorporate commercial production into a land-based economy, and introduce the idea of nationhood. Yet the new art did little to alter the stereotype of the Inuit as "Noble Savages." Hard and elemental, simple in form and conception, stone carvings of animals and Inuit men and women evoked a barren landscape, harsh weather conditions, and a simple close-to-nature lifestyle. Lacking any sense of perspective and little sense of time, the sticklike figures floating on the surface of an Inuit print reinforced the belief that their makers were childlike, anonymous, uneducated, innocent, and therefore in need of protection.

If anyone was duped into believing that Inuit art represented these things, it was not the Inuit who made the objects, but the southern Canadians who bought them. In this sense the stereotype served the Inuit well when it came to marketing their art. For no potential buyer would have wanted to know that most Inuit were now living in the White-dominated settlements and not on the land; that it was not unusual for a family of eight to be crowded into a twelve-by-twenty-four-foot government-issued matchbox house; or that Inuit children wore holsters over their parkas; or, above all, that men and women were carving, drawing, and sewing so that they could provide sufficient food and clothing for their families.

ALL THIS CHARLES GIMPEL knew well. He knew that the production of souvenirs was vital to a "people living on the border of starvation" and insisted that "any activity that can bring them economic stability is to be encouraged."[38] He knew that the Inuit rated an elaborate and sophisticated carving higher than a simple and abstract one simply because "the former is more saleable."[39] He was also aware that the contemporary sculpture and print were not necessarily products of the artist's closeness to nature or a representative of his or her traditional beliefs or ways of life. "Certainly for a number of years," Gimpel wrote, "carvings have been produced with a commercial aim as a market is now available." Above all Gimpel knew that Inuit art would "not continue to flourish indefinitely because no art from any culture has ever done so."[40]

Nevertheless, when Charles undertook his second and third trips to the Canadian Eastern Arctic in the springs of 1961 and 1962, it was for the purpose of collecting Inuit art. Building on the success of his London exhibition in 1959, *The Canadian Eastern Arctic,* and on his show of pre-Columbian art held the following year, Gimpel purchased carvings, drawings, and prints from the West Baffin Eskimo Co-operative, from Bill Hall at Lake Harbour, and from Peter Murdoch at the Rehabilitation Centre at Frobisher Bay. During the early 1960s this work was exhibited alongside his photographs at his London gallery, and other cities in England, as well as in Paris, Zurich, Jerusalem. Though every show was a critical and popular success, the enterprise was far from lucrative.[41] The cost of shipping work out of the Arctic was both high and risky. Prints could be rolled or shipped out flat but carvings were fragile; in an era before bubble-wrap, breakages were frequent. But realizing vast profits was clearly not Gimpel's object. As he told an official at the National Museum of Canada in Ottawa, he promoted Eskimo art in Europe "mainly for the benefit of the Eskimo."[42] Indeed funds resulting from the sale of Inuit art went back into the community via a "scholarship fund for Eskimos proceeding to higher education" which Gimpel set up in 1962.[43]

In 1961 Gimpel was not the tourist-photographer he had been in 1958. Nor was he visiting the Arctic at the end of the summer. And he was certainly not confined to short "Big Ship Time" visits in Frobisher Bay and Cape Dorset. He travelled by airplane from Montreal to Frobisher Bay. There he spent a few days visiting artists at the Rehabilitation Centre, observing the rehearsal of a half-hour CBC radio play produced in Inuktitut, and attending a dance at the Community Hall where he took a memorable photograph of Saqpiniq, a boy from the High Arctic. Then he flew to Cape Dorset where he spent the bulk of his time. Accompanied by James Houston and the Inuit guide and hunter Kov Parr, he made his first journey to the camps by dog sled. In camp Tasiujaqjuaq he photographed Kov's parents in their sod house, and Kov's son Jolly Parr, as he played the accordion. Back in Cape Dorset he photographed Shooyoo, Josephine, Qavavau and Annie, the wife and children of the printmaker Kananginak, who was then president of the West Baffin Eskimo Co-operative. Following the example of Flaherty and Pitseolak he photographed Simeonie Kopapik, who was then a janitor at the school; he caught a group of children playing on a sled; and finally, he visited Kingwatsiak and his daughter Anna who lived in an artificial snowhouse (*elovigarguak*). (In 1956 the Canadian government sent five styrofoam snow-houses, designed by James Houston, to Baffin Island. Though praised as wind- and water-proof and above all warm, they were highly flammable. Kingwatsiak suffered an excruciating death when the one he lived in caught fire.)

Gimpel complained in letters home to his friends that his photography was a bit rusty when he arrived in Cape Dorset in 1961. But the photographs taken during his trips in 1961 and 1962 have enormous documentary value. This is because he not only caught the life in the camps but charted the phenomenal rise of art production in Cape Dorset and in Frobisher Bay: James Houston printing, cutting mats, and viewing drawings in the print studio; Iyola Kingwatsiak making a stone-cut; Quppapik carving out of doors; Eeqeevudluk working on a linocut; and Lucy contemplating a drawing in the privacy of her home. While travelling on the floe edge by sled to hunt seals or to pull arctic char from a frozen lake, Gimpel discovered the aesthetic possibilities of photographing what he called "this world of ice and snow, white glare and cold winds." But travelling in the North was no picnic: "I have dressed very warmly," he wrote home to his wife, Kay, "but then the wind gets its own back by lacerating one's face which makes the nose run which in turn creates icicles."[44] Gimpel's visits in the springs of 1961 and 1962 gave him a taste of what was to come when he returned three years later and made his remarkable journey to Inuksugasalik Point.

Lucy drawing in her home in
Cape Dorset, 3 May 1962

Inuit carvings in the Eskimo Craft Centre,

May 1962

James Houston in front of the

printing press, April 1962

Rehearsing for a radio play at the CBC.

From left to right: Elijah Menarik, Abe Okpik, Leah Idlout,

Peter Murdoch, and Simeonie Michael, Frobisher Bay, 6 May 1961

Simeonie Michael and Elijah Menarik
prompting a husky to supply sound effects for a CBC play,
Frobisher Bay, 6 May 1962

An Inuk woman with her child
at the Rehabilitation Centre in Frobisher Bay,
12 May 1961

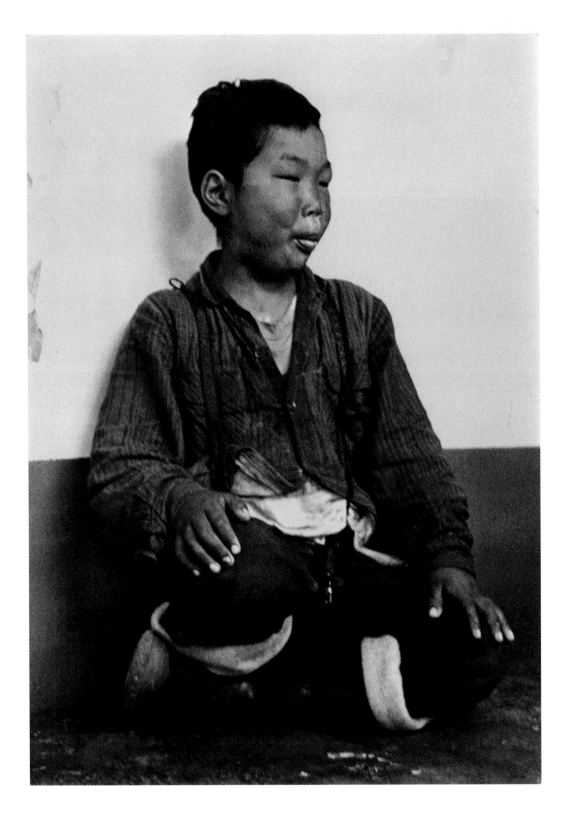

Saqpiniq in the Community Hall at
Frobisher Bay, 13 May 1961

Ron Jones, Pitseolala (who was the medicine woman
in the film *The White Dawn*), and Don Fergusson performing
in the Community Hall at Frobisher Bay, 6 May 1961

On the trail to Lake Harbour, April 1962

Taqiasuk bending over his sled in Cape Dorset,

24 May 1961

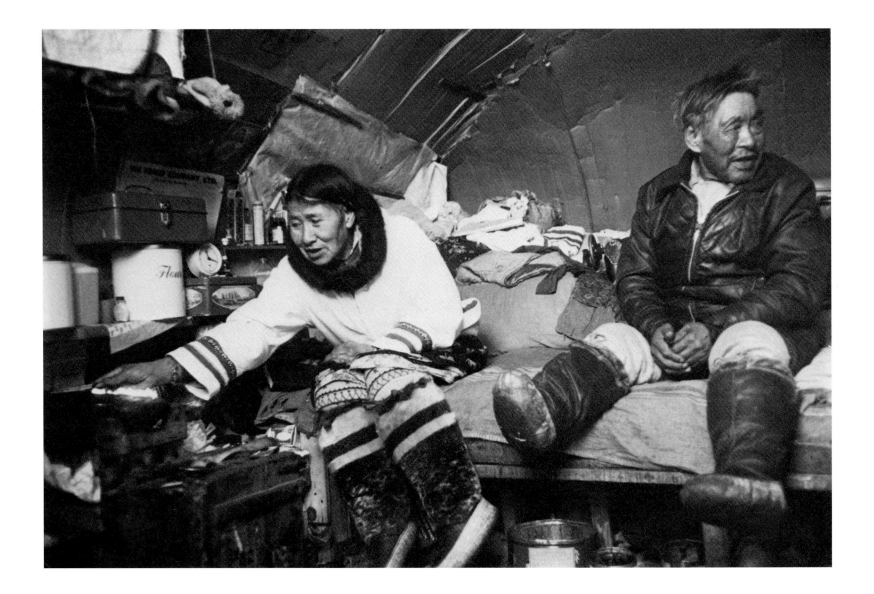

Elisooshee and Parr, the parents of Kov

at Tasiujaqjuaq, 28 April 1962

Kov and Novoalia on a sled, May 1962

Children playing on a sled in Cape Dorset,

2 May 1962

Checking fish nets at Kov's camp,

Tasiujaqjuaq, 20 May 1961

Fishing for arctic char, 28 April 1962

Kov Pudlat seal hunting on floe edge,
Cape Dorset, April 1962

Seal hunting, Cape Dorset, 3 May 1962

Kingwatsiak in the artificial snowhouse in
which he was burned to death,
Cape Dorset, 23 May 1961

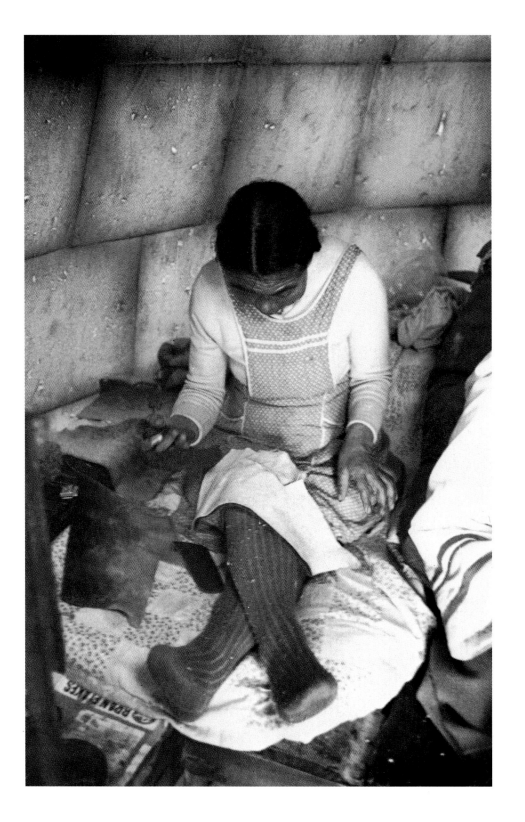

Anna, the daughter of Kingwatsiak, sewing

Charles Gimpel's sealskin boots (kamiik),

Cape Dorset, 23 May 1961

Jolly Parr, Kov's son, playing the accordion
at Tasiujaqjuaq, 28 April 1962

Simeonie Kopapik looking at one of Charles

Gimpel's photographs in Cape Dorset,

17 May 1961

Terry Ryan in Cape Dorset, 25 May 1961

PART III

ON THE TRAIL

It started in New York, March 1964, on a business trip, and I was on my way north. I was having a meal with Jim Houston in his club on top of a building around 56th and 5th Avenue. I was trying to induce Jim to accompany me to Cape Dorset. . . . He, however, had other plans, but being a very kind person he did not want to disappoint me brutally. So without committing himself, he performed a psychological diversion which he knows by experience always works on me. He dangled in front of me the words Inuksugasalik Point: a possibly exciting archaeological site never yet seen by a white man. He himself had tried to get to it but had never managed to do so. He was quite sure of its reality because of numerous Eskimo reports.

"I swallowed the bait and quite forgot to enquire if he would join me. Later it dawned on me that he had not mentioned coming up with me. But by then it did not seem quite so urgent . . . I even had a secret vision of claiming the glory all to myself: that is, if there existed a site, if I did find it and if no other white man had been there before. . . .

"Jim had given me the names of several Eskimos as possible guides; I had other ideas. Ever since my first stay in Cape Dorset I had become very friendly with Kovianaktuliaq Parr – or Kov for short. His family consisted of his wife, Ikuma, tiny and fragile, an unusually small-boned delicate woman for that part of the world; his teenage daughter and two sons. The younger boy was named Jolly the apple of Kov's eye and the most spoilt child I have ever seen even by Eskimo standards. His father-in-law completed the family unit.

"So Kov was to be my guide – but I needed an interpreter too. There are not many in Cape Dorset. On the other visits I had as a teacher Pingwartok, a fourteen-year-old boy, roundheaded with the flatest of flat faces. A keen sense of humour, a very entertaining mixture of deference and cheekiness – he would have been a good travelling companion. But he was still at school . . . so I decided to take Joanasie Salomonie, a young married man who had learned English when he lived further south. Pingwartok was disappointed, but man that he already nearly was, he displayed no emotion.

"The problem was to find our way to the site and back again; Kov who knew of the place had not been there since boyhood. I was nervous of the outcome but he seemed unperturbed. The factors to be estimated were time and food. Kov was speaking of a journey of three days in all; I had a possible flight out to Frobisher Bay six days later – so we had to get away quickly. . . . Journeys anywhere and especially in the Arctic often take longer than planned. Kov and Joanasie had said they would take their own food; but I had earlier learnt that Eskimos not only enjoy their own food, but mine as well on these trips. As I don't appreciate theirs, I double or triple my own rations.

"On the 19th of April we three met at the West Baffin Eskimo Co-operative to choose tinned food for the three of us, based on a three day trip. As things turned out this proved as usual inadequate. How was I to know that the trip was to be extended to four days and that there was an extra team going with us — a fact never mentioned to me out shopping.

"Finally to set the departure time for the following morning, Kov as the owner of the dog team and the guide, suggested 10 a.m. In the north no one ever leaves on time, even less an Eskimo; so I laughed and assured Kov that I would turn up at 10:30 — so I did.

"To my great surprise no dog team was at the rendezvous: to my horror I was told Kov had already left. I could not believe that he would do such a thing, then I realised that he and his dog team were over the ice barrier, waiting for me on the sea ice half a mile away. He was showing that it was the white man, not the Eskimo, who could not be punctual . . . .[1]

Charles Gimpel, 1964

THE TREK TO INUKSUGASALIK Point marked the climax of Charles Gimpel's journeys in the Canadian Eastern Arctic. This was because it was the first time he had made an extensive trip onto the land without a non-Native companion. (He himself noted that "the presence of another white man" would have meant that he "was still an apprentice."[2]) There was "the thrill of covering ground so far unnamed." And, finally, there was the excitement of being the first "white man" to visit, what Gimpel felt must certainly be "one of the most spectacular archaeological sites in the Arctic."[3]

If the weather co-operates, the sixty-mile journey from Cape Dorset to Inuksuga-salik Point is a fourteen-hour ride by Ski-Doo or a one-and-a-half-day trek by dog team. Located on the most western part of the Foxe Peninsula and covering some 250 by 450 yards, the area was once the site of two hundred and fifty Inuksuiit. Today less than half that number are clustered in two groups. The most prominent covers the summit of a rocky promontory that separates the two bays defining the point. The less obvious group is nestled into a gully that slopes towards the sea. Some Inuksuiit are little more than cairns, while "others are works of art, rough stone arranged, balanced and wedged with small supporting rocks." They vary from two to five feet in height; some are composed simply of two rocks; others are more complex structures with windows through the centre and platforms on the top.[4]

In Inuktitut, Inuksuk (the singular form of Inuksuiit) means "in the likeness of man." The Inuksuiit have functioned as markers along caribou migration routes, as places to store food, and, as their name implies, as decoys in aiding the hunting of caribou. People disagree on the origins and purpose of the Inuksuiit at Inuksugasalik Point. Pauta Saila of Cape Dorset, who once lived north of the area, thinks that they were a navigational aid, guiding Inuit sailors through the treacherous waters lying between the Foxe Peninsula and Southampton Island. Brian Lewis, a long-time resident of Iqaluit, has chosen to imbue the place with more mystical meaning. He suggested in the *Canadian Geographical Journal* in 1966 that Inuksuiit were "offerings to the sea-spirits to ensure them safety on the water."[5]

Plagued by poor weather conditions during his short visit to this northern acropolis, Gimpel managed to do only "a very superficial job" of photographing, measuring, and mapping a small group of Inuksuiit located on the highest point of the rocky promontory. In order to help him distinguish one from another he named them after his Innuk guides, Kov Parr, Joanasie Salomonie, and their relatives. Though his visit was, according to his own account, much too brief, it did make him realize that "this site could be of value to Cape Dorset the day tourists go in." Impressed as much by the artistic qualities of the Inuksuiit as by their archaeological value, Gimpel believed that they could be appreciated as art objects and thus provide Inuit artists with further employment. "Properly handled on both sides" of the Atlantic, he told Terry Ryan, who arrived at the Eskimo Craft Centre in the early 1960s, "there should be a great future in the Inukshuks [sic] built by Cape Dorset

Eskimos." When Gimpel returned to Cape Dorset from his monumental journey he therefore commissioned the construction of five for export. He also asked Terry Ryan to give
him exclusive selling rights for two years.[6] Two of the five Inuksuiit were shipped to collec-
tors in the United States; one was reassembled in Gimpel's cottage garden in Suffolk, England.[7]

But the trek to Inuksugasalik Point and the subsequent commissioning of Inuksuiit
were not the only activities that occupied Gimpel on his trip in 1964. There were further
purchases of art works, mainly prints and sculptures, scheduled for exhibition at the Zurich
branch of Gimpel Fils at the end of the year. And, as had become Charles's custom, there
was the taking of more photographs. During this and a subsequent visit to Cape Dorset in
the spring of 1966, Gimpel made a comprehensive record of life in the fast-disappearing
camps. At Igalaalik, a camp of some thirty-six people, he captured Qaqyuraqyuk in the
process of skinning a white fox; Ohituk balancing a ship's biscuit in one hand and an enamel mug in the other during a tea-break; and Nungusuitok playing out of doors. At the much
smaller camp of Itilliarjuk Gimpel photographed Kov building his shelter for the night – a
snowhouse – and Kenojuak with her new baby. In Cape Dorset itself he recorded a broad
range of Native and non-Native activities. With the aid of a flash he photographed Bill Hall
– Angajuqqaakallaapik or small boss man – in his Hudson's Bay Company office; Roy Lucas
– Lucassikallak or short Lucas – in the midst of the West Baffin Eskimo Co-operative store
which he managed; and Kananginak teaching Eqaluk, Pitseolak, and Pee the art of silk-
screen printing at the Eskimo Craft Centre. Out of doors he captured Pitseolak sorting out
the sealskin traces of his dog team then, later, drinking a mug of tea behind a wind-protec-
tive wall of snow blocks. Most of his artistic energy, however, was saved for the journey to
Inuksugasalik Point. Though some of his film was destroyed – film becomes brittle and
breaks in sub-zero weather – he recorded the trip from the moment he left Cape Dorset
for Inuksugasalik Point. Taking a tea-break, checking the trap lines, sorting out the fighting
huskies, building snowhouses, cracking the dog-team whip, mapping the Inuksuiit, icing

the runners of a sled, and leaving Inuksugasalik Point in the early light of dawn inspired some of Gimpel's best photographs.

It was at this time that Gimpel reinforced his image among the Inuit as "this man who was always taking photographs." It was also now that the Inuit of Cape Dorset had an opportunity to see what kind of photographs Gimpel was taking, since he brought a number of prints from his earlier trips with him. Asked what he thought Gimpel was attempting to accomplish in them, Iyola Kingwatsiak replied that "Ukjuk was trying to record how the community was started with the Co-op especially." According to Joanasie Salomonie, Gimpel was "searching for something original." Kov Parr, who was impressed by the fact that Ukjuk could take photographs "that were just right" while bumping and shaking on the back of a sled, believes that Gimpel was attempting "to make people understand the Inuit way of life."

Gimpel's reputation among the residents of Cape Dorset was not limited to his photographic skill. It was on this trip that he appeared publicly in sub-zero weather wearing just his trousers, his skin boots (*kamiik*), and his school tie. "Was he trying to show off to his people that he could survive the cold up here?" Pitaloosie Saila wondered when she reflected on this astonishing incident. Or, as Mikkigak Pee mused, "maybe he had just woken up." Whatever prompted Charles to do such a thing, he is still remembered thirty years later among the elders of Cape Dorset as a "comedian," as "a crazy man," and as someone who "was always joking around."

Igalaalik camp near Cape Dorset, April 1964

Pisutti playing her accordion at
Igalaalik camp, April 1964

Kov Parr building a snowhouse at
Itilliarjuk camp, 28 April 1966

KOV PARR SITS at the kitchen table of house number one hundred in Cape Dorset. The view from the window is commanding because it captures the full sweep of the beach and the opposite shore of Mallik Island. Once a famed hunter and trapper, Kov is now confined to his home by ill health. He still looks strong and is very animated when he speaks, but there is no fishing for char, hunting for seal, or trapping for fox now. Kov was Gimpel's closest Inuit friend: "We understood each other. We were comfortable with each other," and, he adds, "I used to get bored when I wasn't around Ukjuk." Since Charles only knew a few phrases in Inuktitut, the two men had to communicate through an interpreter – though as James Houston pointed out, words were not always necessary because "Eskimos have a subtle way of hearing unheard sounds beyond language, and in that way they immediately sensed the humaneness of Charles."[8] That "humaneness" was, as Kov demonstrated by recalling an incident that took place during their trip to Inuksugasalik Point in 1964, based upon humour. Just as Kov had tried to outwit Charles by turning up early for their rendezvous, now Charles took the opportunity to tease Kov by making him run hard to keep up with the sled. "When I got off the sled and ran alongside it," Kov recalled, "Ukjuk took off with the dogs, then he would let me catch up, before taking off again. I was sweating like hell; it was very frustrating trying to keep up."

Gimpel's relationship with his guides and interpreters was not only built upon humour but upon a good deal of tolerance and mutual respect. "Everything we would do," Joanasie Salomonie recalled, "he would do." And while according to Kov, "he ate just like everyone else and this was very rare," Charles continued to profess a distaste for Inuit country food. Aware of this, Kov and Joanasie once disguised raw walrus meat as caribou in order to make it more palatable to their friend. "Charles did not know until after that it was walrus," Joanasie laughed when he recalled the incident.

Gimpel also won his Inuit companions over by recalling many of his harrowing experiences during the Second World War. Though he was known back in England for his reluctance to talk about those experiences, Charles was surprisingly forthcoming to both his Native and non-Native friends in the North. He told Terry Ryan that he was so badly beaten in the concentration camp that it was impossible for him to escape as he had done on earlier occasions.[9] And what he shared with his interpreter Joanasie, who was fascinated to meet someone who had been in the war, "was very sad, horrible."

THE FIRST EXHIBITION of Inuit carvings and prints to be mounted in Zurich opened on December 10, six months after Charles had returned to Europe. Gimpel had given a lecture the night before "at the best art club" in Zurich in order to prepare his audience for the show. As a result the private view was well attended. There was a good press, adequate television coverage, and though the Canadian ambassador had missed the opening, he made a discreet appearance the following day. Above all, the sales were good. This allowed Gimpel to note with pleasure that for the first time the operating expenses of shipping art from the Canadian Eastern Arctic would be covered.[10]

The climate in England and in North America was looking equally good for Inuit art. An exhibition of Inuit art, accompanied by Charles's photographs, opened in the new year at a gallery in Sunderland in the north of England. A further collection of Gimpel's photographs was mounted at the Explorer's Hall in Washington, D.C. that autumn. Sponsored by the National Geographical Society and put on tour under the auspices of the Smithsonian Institution's Traveling Service, the exhibition moved to Winnipeg in the new year, then to eight other venues across North America. *The Eskimo in a Changing World* received, without exception, good reviews.[11]

Following his trip to the Arctic in 1964 Charles decided to hand over a large part of his Inuit art collection – it consisted of stone-cuts, etchings, drawings, and sculptures – to the Scott Polar Research Institute in Cambridge, England. The Institute had just been awarded a Ford Foundation grant to extend its premises. A larger building meant that there would be adequate space in which to put Gimpel's collection on permanent display. The collection, however, was not to be far out of Charles's reach. As he told Alma Houston, "I will be able to borrow for exhibition purposes."[12]

Gimpel not only gave away his own collection, but encouraged others to donate work to the Scott Polar Research Institute in order to make it "the most important Canadian Eskimo art centre in the world – outside of Canada."[13] Though this act of generosity seemed to mark the end of Gimpel's passion for collecting, he was back in Cape Dorset for a short visit in 1966 and then, despite his deteriorating health, again in 1968. This, his last trip, was to yield a very different collection of photographs.

Kenojuak and her baby at Itilliarjuk camp,

April 1964

Qaqyuraqyuk in the first and second stages
of skinning a fox, Igalaalik camp,
29 April 1966

Ohituk drinking tea and eating a "ship's biscuit"
in Qaqyuraqyuk's home at Igalaalik camp,
29 April 1966

Nungusuitok in front of a sled at
Igalaalik camp, 16 April 1964

Kananginak teaching Eqaluk, Pitseolak, and

Pee how to make a silk-screen print,

Cape Dorset, April 1966

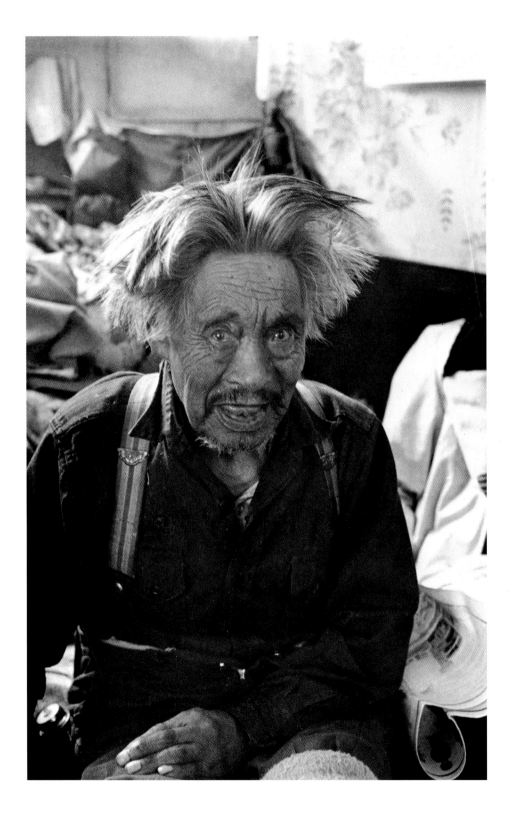

Parr, Cape Dorset, 5 May 1966

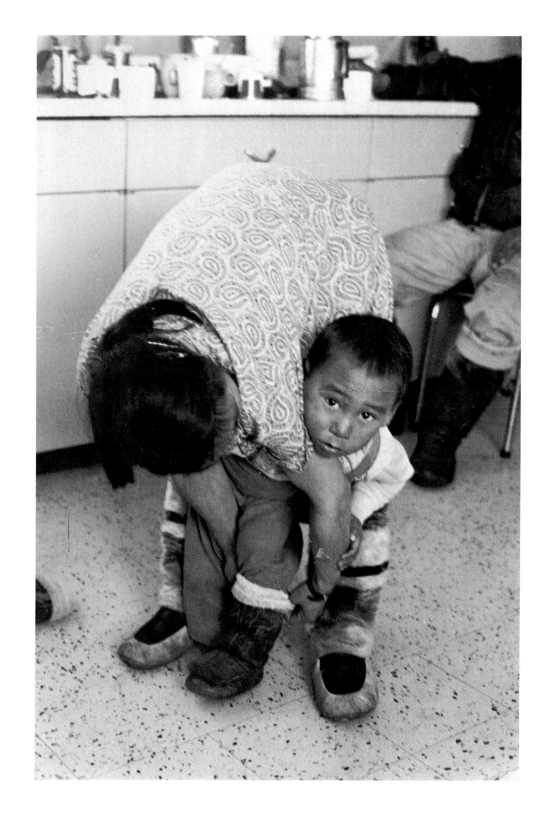

Nipisa, the wife of Oshuitok Ipeelee,
and their son Sangani, Cape Dorset,
April 1964

Roy Lucas, or Lucassikallak (short Lucas), at
the West Baffin Eskimo Co-operative,
Cape Dorset, 27 April 1964

Uqsuralik feeding her child in the
West Baffin Eskimo Co-operative,
Cape Dorset, 16 April 1964

Pitseolak having just returned from checking his fox line near
Cape Dorset sorts out the sealskin traces
of his dog team, 17 April 1964

Kov Parr suffocating a white fox by
stepping on its lungs, 21 April 1964

First day on the trail: packing up the sled in
Cape Dorset, 19 April 1964

Second day on the trail: dogs fighting,

20 April 1964

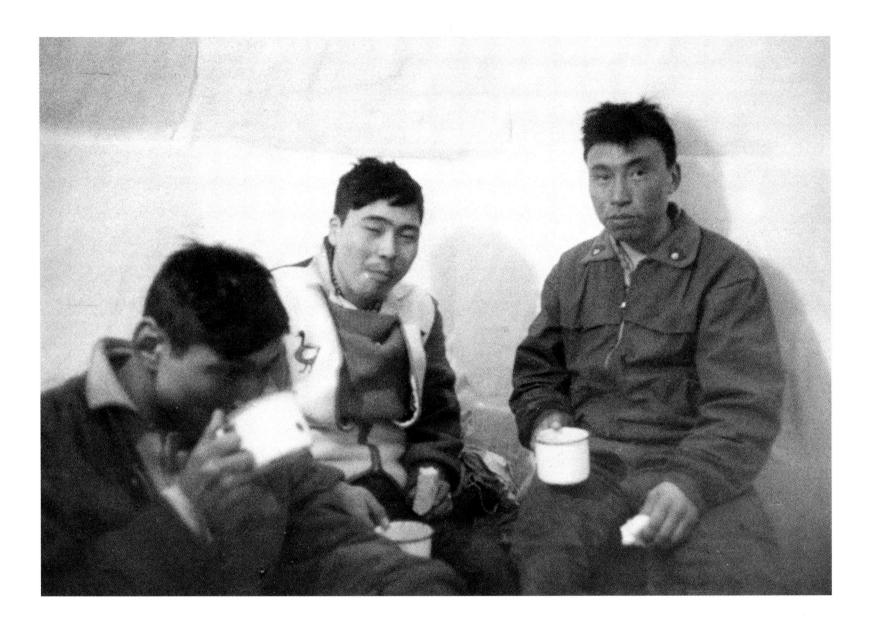

Second day on the trail: Kov, Joanasie, and
Qaboroq in snowhouse, 20 April 1964

Fourth day on the trail: view from the entrance of

a snowhouse; Kov icing the runners of the sled,

22 April 1964

Tea break on the trail towards
Inuksugasalik Point, April 1964

Inuksuiit at Inuksugasalik Point, 21 April 1964

Inuksuk built by Kov between Cape Dorset
and Itilliarjuk, 28 April 1966

Leaving Inuksugasalik Point in the early

morning, April 1964

PART IV

LIVING BOTH
WAYS

I decided to make a two-day trip to some Eskimo camps to condition my weary city bones . . .

Oshuitok Ipeelee, formerly Jim Houston's right hand man, who was to be my host and guide, decided

to take his mechanical sledge as well as a small dog team. The going out was perfect: sun bright with

no wind, both sledges giving good performances according to their standards, i.e. the mechanical

sledge running slightly faster than the dog team who nearly burst their guts to keep up with this

seemingly unfair competition.

"The next day the weather turned colder, the snow fell making progress that much more difficult. In the afternoon when my body was beginning to rebel against all this unnecessary exertion (and I abhor the cold), the perishing motor started breaking down. My vision of savouring a hot bath and a cooked European dinner within the next few hours faded. Every time a breakdown occurred, it seemed hours before Oshuitok got the thing working again. Meanwhile halts were freezing me into a semi-stupor of agony, made all the worse because I remembered the new horror stories then circulating in the Arctic. How the silly Eskimos relying on these new machines travelled on them: any breakdown left them helpless in the wilderness to die of hunger and cold, not even able to eat dogs for a last meal.

"Our predicament was not quite so bad – in fact in retrospect and remembering it in a warm room, it was just an annoying incident, but at the time I felt a cross between Scott and Franklin. Two hours' distance from Cape Dorset, the engine, by then running smoothly, once again broke down – this time simply for lack of petrol. Petrol pumps being what they are not in that area, we abandoned ship and all climbed onto the already over-crowded sledge pulled by the dog team. Even in my helpless and miserable state of mind and body I tried to make a joke about riding in a full bus at the rush hour. But it fell flat possibly because of the translation into Eskimo or more probably because a bus, let alone a bus at the rush hour, is beyond their experience. The huskies had the last howl but any satisfaction was lost in their strenuous effort to drag us home very slowly. We finally made Dorset long after midnight; exhausted, miserable and cold I crawled into bed."[1]

Charles Gimpel, 1964

Previous page: Adamie's son Novoalia with his carvings in the textile shop, Cape Dorset, 1 April 1968

The self-propelled sled first appeared in the Arctic in 1927. This prototype was cumbersome and slow. An air-cooled, two-cycle, lightweight engine was developed in the early 1950s to overcome the problem of a high weight-to-power ratio. Then, in 1955, Bombardier put the first Ski-Doos, or snowmobiles as they were also called, onto the market;

they produced 255 that first year and sold them for one thousand dollars each.[2] By the late 1960s Bombardier's total Ski-Doo sales were well over 110,000. In just over ten years the mechanical sled had become the most favoured means of transportation in the Arctic.

Snowmobiles were much faster than dog sleds. They had a greater carrying capacity, did not have to be "fed," made possible a one-day excursion onto the land instead of a three-day trek, and spared the driver from the second-hand smell of walrus meat which was blown back by the dogs. But as Charles Gimpel discovered during his two-day journey to Igalaalik with Oshuitok Ipeelee, there were disadvantages too. Snowmobiles frequently broke down. Maintenance and repairs were costly. They were noisy. No match for a dog team at the floe edge, their popularity contributed to the decline in the hunt for marine mammals. And most important of all, as Gimpel so rightly observed, the Ski-Doo could not become food to sustain the stranded hunter.

The Inuit had little choice but to adopt this new means of transportation. In 1962 the dog population in Pangnirtung had been decimated by a distemper epidemic. And in Cape Dorset, Arctic Bay, and other settlements on Baffin Island, the imposition of a law preventing dogs from running loose caused the canine population to drop in an equally dramatic fashion. If the dogs ran free, they were destroyed: "Father cried when the RCMP shot his dogs," Katauga Saila of Cape Dorset recalled. If they were tied up, they became weak from lack of exercise, or froze to death, or starved. Consequently the dogs, as Konoo Muckpaloo of Arctic Bay remembered, were "in very bad shape."[3]

The almost universal use of the snowmobile was just one example of the way in which the Inuit were coerced into adopting southern technology. The advent of scheduled flights to remote Arctic communities such as Cape Dorset was another. While regular airline service eliminated the scramble for supplies previously made available by the once-a-year government and Hudson's Bay Company supply ships, they increased the dependence of the Inuit upon imported goods. The seemingly benevolent expansion of government-sponsored social services in the Arctic had an increasingly dependent-making effect on the

Inuit, too. And the representation of an Inuk – it was Gimpel's interpreter, Joanasie Salomonie – on the Northwest Territories Council in 1966 made their incorporation into the Euro-Canadian hegemony complete.

When Gimpel made his last trip to Baffin Island in 1968 it was evident that the government's attempt to impose a westernized lifestyle on the Inuit had run into difficulties. The public outcry against the killing of baby seals had thrown the sealing industry into disarray. The introduction of an individualist money-based economy alongside traditional hunting practices based on sharing left the Inuit, as Hugh Brody observed, "somewhere at the crossroads between wage labourer, land owner, and complete resourcelessness."[4] As a result, fifty per cent of the Inuit were on relief. The health and welfare of the Inuit was not much better: their mortality rate was far above the national average. Incidents of spree-drinking and home-brew making were, according to the resident Royal Canadian Mounted Police officer, on the rise.[5] And the educational system was a failure. Most Inuit never entered high school; those who did had no way of applying what they learned there once they returned to their community.

Yet few Inuit would have readily forfeited the goods and services they obtained from the South. "I'm happy about having white man's food when you want it," Peter Pitseolak told Dorothy Eber in the late 1960s, "and I'm happy about having a place to live where the heat is always the same."[6] However, most Inuit, including Peter Pitseolak, would have agreed with Muckpaloo's observation that their dependence upon these things "all happened so fast;"[7] As a result, they were, as Maata Pudlat of Cape Dorset put it, "caught between." "I don't know how to be Inuk," she told the oral historian Mary Crnkovich, "and I know the white's way of life, but that will never make me a white, so I am in between, I am living both ways."[8]

The Inuit feelings of anomie, of belonging to neither one nor the other culture to the point of living in between the two, not only arose from the attempt by southern Canadians to re-make the Inuit in their own image. It was also a product of the southern

Canadians' relentless comparison of the Inuit to the stereotype of the happy-go-lucky, uncomplaining, and self-sufficient "Eskimo" that they had created in their films, photographs, memoirs, and through other media. This view functioned in two ways: at a distance the "strangers" admired Inuit art; at close quarters they measured every Inuk man and woman they encountered against the ideal "Eskimo" type. So while some Euro-Canadians sought to make the Inuit like themselves, others were content to leave them in the wilderness.

The extent to which the Inuit have been affected by the policies and attitudes that have emerged from these conflicting points of view is evident in the home of Abe Okpik, a translator, broadcaster, and writer originally from the Western Arctic but now a resident of Iqaluit. Hanging from a nail on the living-room wall of his small house is Abe's identification disc. (Until 1971 the Canadian government required all Inuit to wear around their necks metal discs stamped with their number.) Next to it is a photograph. In it Abe is dressed in black tie. The photograph was taken at Rideau Hall five years after Abe had hung up his disc. It marks the occasion when Abe received the Order of Canada for his services as an interpreter for Justice Thomas Berger on the Mackenzie Valley Pipeline Inquiry and for the significant role he played in "Operation Surname," the project that assigned the Inuit with "proper" surnames to replace their numerical identifications.

Kov and Ikuma Parr looking at Charles's
photographs at Tasiujaqjuaq camp,
April 1968

Epirvik and a friend unloading a Nordair
aircraft at Cape Dorset, March 1968

During his final visit to Cape Dorset in April of 1968 Charles Gimpel was aware of the tensions that were pulling the Inuit back to their old ways as well as making them more dependent on the southern lifestyle offered in the permanent settlements. As Maata Pudlat told Mary Crnkovich, "I try to go out on the land as much as possible with my children, [because] that's where I have good feelings"[9] Gimpel was sensitive to the realization by the Inuit that they possessed a distinct heritage. This awareness had arisen partly as a result of the making and the reception of Inuit art.[10] It also had a lot to do with their association with the native rights movement in Canada, which led to the founding in Pangnirtung on Baffin Island of the Inuit Tapirisat of Canada. Founded in 1971, "the people's team" as it was also called, was the country's first national Inuit organization.

Not surprisingly Gimpel's last photographs reflect the tensions between the new and the old ways. A Nordair aircraft delivers a sack full of potatoes to Cape Dorset. Two sleds are pulled by Ski-Doos. Inuit artists print on fabric. Many of the people in his photographs are dressed entirely in imported clothing; some use southern appliances, sit on Western furniture; and one of them displays his Order of Canada medal.[11] Equally these last photographs convey the continuation of "old ways": raising children in the hood of a parka, prettying a fox pelt, sleeping on a platform in a tent or sod house, carving in stone, and living on the land. By juxtaposing and more often by mixing these opposing lifestyles, Gimpel was not only showing the extent to which the Inuit were living between two cultures, he was challenging the belief, endemic among the non-Native community long before his first visit to the Arctic in 1958, that the Inuit would not survive the technological, cultural, social, and political invasion from the South. Above all, Charles was giving visual evidence that the Inuit were following the course set out by Abe Okpik in 1962: "If we can think like our ancestors and put to use what they have achieved for us, and adopt the white man's way of learning at the same time and keep our own way," Okpik wrote in the magazine *North,* "we will be further ahead."[12]

Gimpel was capable of seeing the present and future of the Inuit, of glimpsing between the cracks because he was no longer simply a tourist-photographer out for an adventure. During the 1960s he had become a friend of the Inuit, a major patron and promoter of their art, a courageous and adaptable companion on the trail, and the comedian of the settlement to boot.

Gimpel's last photographs are a far cry from the mug shots of unevangelized Inuit that peppered the missionary tracts at the turn of the century, or the blurry illustrations of Inuit men and women that enlivened the memoirs of white adventurers and the official reports of explorers and scientists, or the idealized dramatic portraits of silhouetted Inuit hunters so favoured by the pre- and post-Second World War romantic photographers. Gimpel's last photographs even differ from the photographs he took on his first trip. In 1958 he had paid a great deal of attention to composition, detail, and to lighting effects. His Inuit subjects, whom he rarely identified by name, were given plenty of space. He often took a long shot when a close-up one might have been better. And he sometimes fell back upon the visual devices that Flaherty, Harrington, and other photographers had established before him. The result was an impersonal, even cool, record. Only the disarmingly uninhibited and curious children were forthcoming in their response to him.

By contrast, Gimpel's last photographs are highly personal portraits. His earlier interest in types gave way to an obsession with individuals. The space surrounding his subjects was more intimate. He paid less attention to composition and lighting effects. He now preferred the candid shot to the carefully composed one. As James Houston observed, he was probing "for the lights and darks, the contrasts" and searching "for a basic man." By doing these things, Gimpel introduced all of those unfamiliar with the Arctic to "the bleak, bone bare expanses of the Eskimo world."[13]

No longer the unobserved, unseen eye behind the camera, Gimpel, like the Inuit photographer Peter Pitseolak whose photographs he must have seen, was a participating observer. This new complicity with his subjects allowed him to give his magnificent portraits of Parr, Adamie, Axangayuk, and Pee an emotive charge. Equally, it made possible the more subtle and intimate photographs of Kov and Ikuma, of Kananginak and Ping-wartok, and of Kenojuak, Lucy, and Pitseolak. None of the people in these photographs are stereotyped, categorized, or marginalized. None of these works fit into the southern Canadian's ideal of the "Noble Savage" or "Noble Victim." Even when the Inuit are dancing, Gimpel presents them as dignified, self-possessed individuals who are living a life parallel to but definitely separate from their Euro-Canadian dancing partners. By giving his Inuit subjects a future as well as a past, by creating intimate portraits that reflect the full range of their experiences, and by showing the extent to which they were capable of living between two cultures, Gimpel had turned the historic misrepresentation of the Inuit on its head.

In the autumn of 1972 the carver and printmaker Iyola Kingwatsiak flew to London, England in the company of Davidee Qabik, an interpreter from Inukjuak. Though Iyola was the first Cape Dorset Inuk to travel to Europe, he was not among the first Inuk to be put "on show" outside of the Canadian Eastern Arctic. As early as 1501 a Portuguese ship, under the command of Gaspan Cort-Réal, had reputedly taken fifty Inuit, captured off the coast of Labrador, to Europe. In 1566 a young Inuk woman and her child were kidnapped in the same area by French sailors. They sailed to Europe where they were exhibited in a number of cities as "savages."[14] A decade after this, Martin Frobisher brought an Inuk man, his wife, and child from Baffin Island to England. Unable to withstand their new inhospitable environment they soon died.

Iyola's fate was, however, quite different. He was not to become the subject of a crudely cut woodblock handbill announcing that he was on exhibit. Nor was he to be immortalized in the sketches or paintings of the most celebrated European artists of the day. He had come to London to view an exhibition devoted to Inuit art. *Sculpture of the Inuit: Masterworks of the Canadian Arctic* opened at the British Museum in October of 1972.

Organized by the Canadian Arts Council and funded by the Canadian government, it was mounted not only in London and several points across Canada, but in Moscow, Paris, and Copenhagen. It was the grandest international tribute to pre-historic, historic, and contemporary Inuit art, and Iyola had been invited to attend the opening in London. Alma Houston recalled "feeling that the presence of Inuit artists, at each and every opening lent a touch of reality to the wonder of it all."[15]

Iyola is sorry that he cannot remember much about his trip to England: "I should have thought that somebody would ask me some day" was his reply to my questions. But he does recall that "a lot of people stared at him;" that he made sure he "stuck next to somebody" so that he would not get lost; and that he visited the Gimpel Fils Gallery where his work was first shown so many years earlier.

Charles was ill. He had had an operation for cancer in 1970 and his condition was getting worse. Confined to his cottage in Cretingham, he was unable to attend the opening. This saddened Gimpel deeply because on show was the work of Luktak, Oshuitok Ipeelee, along with that of the many other artists he had exhibited in Paris, Zurich, London, and elsewhere long before anyone else.

On christmas day of 1973 Gimpel's two sons, René and Charles, carried their father down the stairs from the bedroom to the sitting room at Ivy Cottage in Cretingham. Gimpel was thus able to spend what Kay remembered as "surely the most wonderful Christmas ever passed by any family." It was to be his last. There followed long, sleepless nights "when the sickroom walls closed in" and Charles, with Kay at his side, "visited far-off places." Then came the day in late January when Charles told Kay "I am defeated; I can fight no longer." He died the next day.

A week after his death Charles was buried in the village graveyard "beneath the tower he so often photographed from across the little valley."[16] And two weeks after that, Robert McKenzie, the political scientist and Canadian-born cousin of Kay, read a memorial service to a large crowd gathered at London's Grosvenor Chapel. After extolling Gimpel's abilities as an amateur photographer and as a professional art dealer, McKenzie attempted to come to grips with Charles's character: "I have a feeling that no-one knew him completely. He was a public man who lived part of his life in an intensely private world, not just with his family, to whom he was intensely devoted, but in 'the cave of his own skull.'"[17]

While Charles might have been somewhat elusive to his friends, the photographs that he took in the Canadian Eastern Arctic during a decade of radical change are anything but vague. They are full of humanity and humour. And they possess a critical edge which enables the viewer, whomever he or she might be, to confront head on the predicament of a people caught between two cultures.

Parr wearing his Order of Canada medal,

Cape Dorset, 29 March 1968

Terry Ryan talking with Kananginak through the interpreter
Pingwartok at the Eskimo Craft Centre, 2 April 1968

Terry Ryan in the textile shop,

Cape Dorset, 2 April 1968

The printmaker Mikkigak Pee in the textile shop,

Cape Dorset, 11 April 1968

The carver Axangayuk in the textile shop,

Cape Dorset, April 1968

Adamie with his carving of a bear in the textile shop, Cape Dorset, 1 April 1968

Oshuitok Ipeelee with one of his carvings,

Cape Dorset, 9 April 1968

Lucy, Kenojuak, and Pitseolak in the
Northern Service Officer's home,
Cape Dorset, 16 April 1968

Top: The printmaker Lucy, Cape Dorset, 16 April 1968

Right: Kenojuak the print maker, Cape Dorset, 16 April 1968

Helen Hall in the Hudson's Bay
Company residence at Cape Dorset,
April 1968

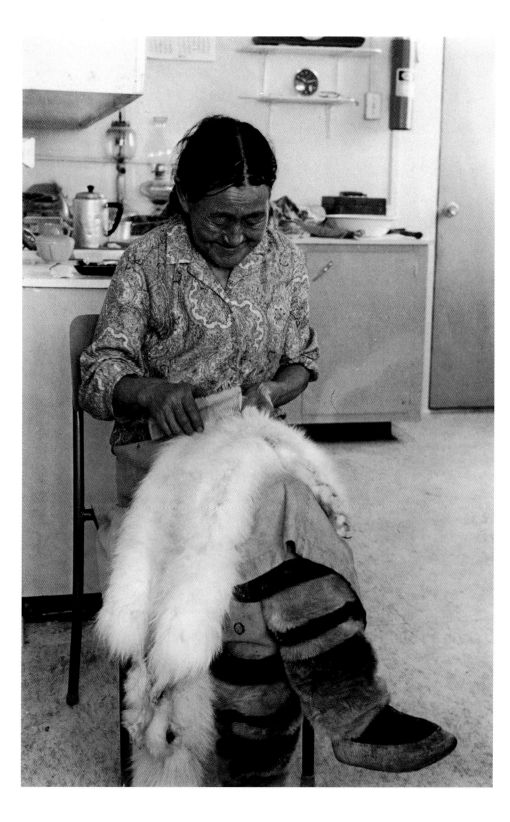

Aggeok, Peter Pitseolak's wife,

prettying a white fox pelt, Cape Dorset,

28 March 1968

Mayoreak with her infant and her son Sappa,

Cape Dorset, 15 April 1968

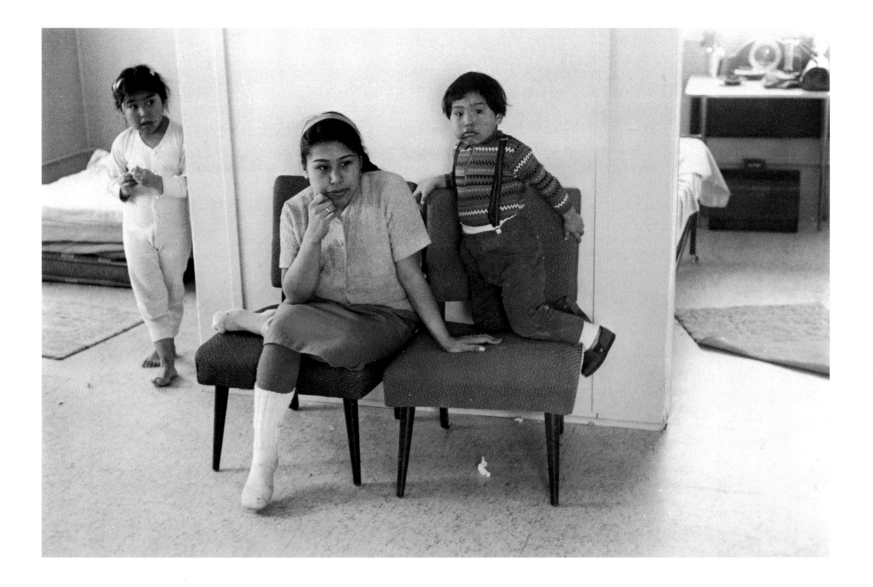

Katauga (the author's interpreter in June 1993),
her mother Pitaloosie, and her brother Matsauja in their
Cape Dorset home, April 1968

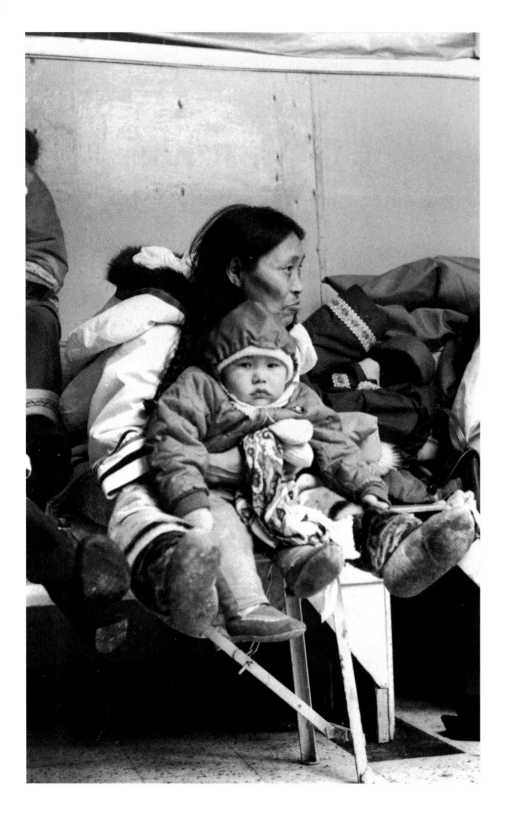

Kimeata with a child at the Friday
evening dance, Cape Dorset,
17 April 1968

Peter Pitseolak, Terry Ryan, and Lenore Stoneberg
at the Friday evening dance, Cape Dorset,
17 April 1968

Terry Ryan, Sororsilutu Onalik, Peter Pitseolak, Pat Ryan,
Kananginak, Alma Houston, and Tommy Manning at the
Friday evening dance, Cape Dorset, 17 April 1968

Peter Pitseolak's son Potoogook with
"Player's" mask, Cape Dorset,
28 March 1968

Kov and Ikuma Parr's daughter Mary
carrying her sister Leah in the hood,
Cape Dorset, 29 March 1968

On the trail out of Inuksugasalik Point, 5 April 1968

Iyola Kingwatsiak at the
Gimpel Fils Gallery in London,
October 1972 (Photographer unknown)

INTRODUCTION

1   Gimpel Fils Gallery Archives (hereafter GFGA)
Charles Gimpel to H. Howith, Department of Northern
Affairs and National Resources, 20 November 1962.
Ernest Richard, who was known as Charles following
World War II, was born 5 August 1913 at Vaucresson,
Haut-de-Seine, France. Of French and English parent-
age (he was the son of René Gimpel and Florence
Duveen, the daughter of Lord Duveen). James Houston
"Ernest Richard Charles Gimpel – Obituary," *Polar
Record,* vol. 16, no. 105 (September 1973), 877.

2   Houston, op. cit., 877.

3   William Bradford, "Account of Author's Cruise to
Davis Strait and Baffin Bay on Panther," *Journal of the
American Geographical Society,* vol. 17 (1885), 79.

4   Houston, op. cit., 877.

5   Franz Boas, *The Central Eskimo,* Smithsonian Institution, U.S. Bureau of Ethnology, Sixth Annual Report
1884–1885 (Washington 1888).

6   Ira Jacknis, "Franz Boas and Photography," *Studies
in Visual Communication,* vol. 10, no. 1 (Winter 1984), 4.
Jacknis writes nothing about Boas's fabrication of the
photographs which appeared in his seminal study of the
Inuit. He does, however, note that Boas did misuse photographs of the Kwakiutl potlaches which had been
"taken with different actors on different days and
places," 39.

7   Douglas Cole, "Franz Boas in Baffin-Land," *The
Beaver* (August/September 1986), 7, 15.

8   Ibid., 15.

9   Agnes Deans Cameron, *The New North; Being Some
Account of a Woman's Journey Through Canada to the Arctic*
(London, 1908); Julian W. Bilby, *Among Unknown Eskimo*
(London 1923); Philip H. Godsell, *Arctic Trader, an
Account of Twenty Years with the Hudson's Bay Company*
(London 1934); and Vilhjalmur Stefansson, *The Friendly
Arctic, the Story of Five Years in Polar Regions* (New York
1921).

10   George Binney, *The Eskimo Book of Knowledge;
Aglait, Iisimatiksat Inungnut Ilingnajut* (London 1931), 4.

11   GFGA, Kay Gimpel to Alice Houston, 5 August
1973.

12   James Houston cited by Robert McKenzie, Memorial Chapel Service, Grosvenor Chapel, London, 15
February 1973.

13   GFGA, "Edward" to Charles Gimpel, Grenfell Hos-
pital, St. Anthony, Newfoundland, 14 March 1946.

14   GFGA, James Houston to Kay Gimpel, 12 July
1973.

15   W.L. Morton, *The Canadian Identity* (Madison,
Wisconsin 1961), 93.

16   Franz Boas had employed this convention in his
publication *The Eskimo of Baffin Land and Hudson Bay* in
1901. This time he included photographs which had
been taken in the Arctic, most probably by his friend
Captain James Mutch. See Boas, *The Eskimo of Baffin
Land and Hudson Bay,* Bulletin of the American Museum
of Natural History, vol. XV, 1901, plates I–IV.

17   Joanna Cohan Scheier, "Introduction: Historical
Photographs as Anthropological Documents: A Retrospect," *Visual Anthropology,* vol. 3, no. 2–3 (1990), 133.

18   Archibald Lang Fleming, *Dwellers in Arctic Night*
(London 1929, first published 1928), 112.

19   See, for example, Father Jean Philippe, "Eskimo
Psychology," *Eskimo,* no. 4 (February 1946), 7. Father
Guy Mary-Rosselierre of Pond Inlet, along with a hand-
ful of other Roman Catholic missionaries, are an exception. According to Renee Wissink, Father Mary
"essentially is an Inuk. He has and continues to live in
the Inuit world." Wissink to author, 14 September
1993.

20   Mary Crnkovich, ed., *"Gossip" A Spoken History of*

Women in the North (Ottawa 1990), 18.

21   Susan Cowan, ed., *We Don't Live in Snow Houses Now; Reflections of Arctic Bay* (Ottawa 1976), 21.

22   "While hunting for seabirds, Taktillitak was carried away by the sea to a very small island where he ran out of food. He built his own grave and lay down to die, but after dreaming of seals he got up and killed a seal with a club. He made a sealskin float, paddled to shore and walked to camp where his friends were so happy to see him they burst into tears." Dorothy Eber, *Peter Pitseolak 1902–1973, Inuit Historian of Seekooseelak* (Montreal 1980), 19.

23   Ibid., 13.

24   When the Hudson's Bay Company's *Beaver* magazine published a selection of his photographs in 1959, they praised him for depicting "the contemporary Eskimo and his family" living in their new permanent homes, working in the mines and on construction sites, and studying in new classrooms. "Journey from the Igloo," *The Beaver* (Spring 1959), 13, 15.

25   GFGA, Kay Gimpel to Alan, 14 July 1973.

26   Houston, op. cit., 878.

27   Author's interview with James Houston, 31 August 1993.

28   Ronald Blythe, *The Times,* 2 February 1973.

29   See, for example, Gontran de Poncins, *Eskimos* (New York 1949) and *Kabloona* (New York 1941) and Richard Harrington, *The Face of the Arctic; a Cameraman's Story in Words and Pictures of Five Journeys into the Far North* (New York 1952), and *Northern Exposures: Canada's Backwoods and Barrens Pictured in Monochrome and Colour by Richard Harrington* (Toronto 1953).

30   Harrington, op. cit., *The Face of the Arctic*, 248.

31   In *The Face of the Arctic* Harrington writes of one starving Padleimiut woman, whom he incorrectly called Padlei, "Although skin is loose on her bones, her artiggi black and without warmth – she still goes on, uncomplaining, at starvation camp near Padlei," 236 .

32   Farley Mowat, *People of the Deer* (London 1952). For a more recent account see Alan Rudolph Marcus, "Utopia on Trial, Perceptions of Canadian government experiments with Inuit relocation" (Cambridge Ph.D. thesis 1994).

33   Author's interview with Dr. Terence Armstrong, 25 February 1993, in Cambridge, England.

34   Julian Bell, "Decency and Delusion," *The Times Literary Supplement*, 19 March 1993, 7.

PART ONE

1   Charles Gimpel, "The Canadian Eskimo in a Changing World" in *Arctic Photographs by Charles Gimpel and Contemporary Eskimo Art,* Gimpel Fils Gallery (London 1961), n.p.

2   Charles Gimpel's library was bequeathed to the West Baffin Eskimo Co-Operative and remains there to this day.

3   Penny Petrone, ed., *Northern Voices, Inuit Writing in English* (Toronto 1988), 167.

4   GFGA, Charles Gimpel "Diary" [1958], 27 August 1958.

5   Ibid., 5 September 1958.

6   Ibid., 6 September 1958.

7   Ibid., 8 September 1958.

8   Ibid., 8 September 1958.

9   Ibid., 9 September 1958.

10   Ibid., 9 September 1958.

11   Hudson's Bay Company Archives, Provincial Archives of Manitoba, RG-7 – unclassified, Captain A.C. Lloyd, "Highlights of Twelve Years on the Rupertsland" (typescript), 7.

12   Gimpel, op. cit., "Diary," 25 August 1958; ibid.,

26 August 1958.

13 Christina cited in *The Globe and Mail,* 24 July 1993; Gimpel, op. cit., "Diary," 5 September 1958.

14 Gimpel, op. cit., "Diary," 26 August 1958.

15 Ibid., 8 September 1958.

16 Ibid., 4 September 1958.

17 Ibid., 7 September 1958.

18 GFGA, Charles Gimpel, "Notebook" [1958].

19 Gimpel, op. cit., "Diary," 1 September 1958.

20 Ibid., 28 August 1958.

21 Ibid., 5 September 1958.

22 Ibid., 27 August 1958.

23 Gimpel, op. cit., "Notebook."

24 Ibid.

25 Ibid., Gimpel to Gus Lueshen, 12 February 1959.

26 GFGA, Charles Gimpel to Frank Walker, 6 November 1958.

27 *The Beaver,* (Spring 1959), 39–47.

28 See Peter Geller's article, "The 'True North' in Pictures?" in *Archivaria,* vol. 36 (Autumn 1993).

29 GFGA, newspaper clippings.

30 Gimpel, op. cit., "Diary," 28 August 1958.

PART TWO

1 Charles Gimpel, "A Collector's View," *The Beaver* (Autumn 1967), 72.

2 This term was used by Erna Gunther in *Art in the Life of the Northwest Coast Indians* (Portland, 1960), "Chapter 11." Jonathan King of the Museum of Mankind in London kindly brought this to my attention.

3 Gimpel, op. cit., 74.

4 The origins of this claim rest on the influence of Gimpel's London exhibition of Inuit Art in 1953. See: Virginia Watt, "In Retrospect," *Inuit Art Quarterly* (Spring 1989) and "Prospects for the Eskimo" *Edmonton*

Journal, 30 July 1953.

5 See Charles A. Martijn's excellent discussion about the origins of contemporary Inuit art in "Canadian Eskimo Carving in Historical Perspective," *Anthropos,* vol. 59 (1964), 546–556.

6 Renee Wissink to author, 14 September 1993.

7 Nelson H.H. Graburn, "Commercial Inuit Art: a Vehicle for the Economic Development of the Eskimos of Canada," *Inter-Nord* no. 15 (December 1978), 132.

8 Jean Blodgett, *Kenojuak* (Toronto 1985), 23.

9 Helga Goetz, *The Role of the Department of Indian and Northern Affairs in the Development of Inuit Art,* Inuit Section, Research and Documentation Centre (Ottawa 1985), 7.

10 From its founding early in the century the Canadian Handicraft Guild (now called the Canadian Guild of Crafts in Quebec, henceforth CGCQ) had been committed to the promotion of Native handicrafts in Canada. The Guild approached the government in 1933, through its president Wilfred Bovey and in 1941 through its Indian and Eskimo Committee. See Morris Zaslow, *The Northward Expansion of Canada 1914–1967* (Toronto 1988), 171 and CGCQ, Alice M.S. Lighthall, "Indian and Eskimo Committee Report, 1941."

11 Houston, *Eskimo Handicrafts* (Montreal 1951).

12 National Archives of Canada, RG85, vol. 387, file 255–5/166 [1], Houston, "Answers to Questions of Arts and Crafts Project, Cape Dorset, 1956."

13 CGCQ, James Houston, "Report on Eskimo Handicraft, Canadian Eastern Arctic, Summer of 1953 via S.S. C.D. Howe."

14 Houston began in 1957 by making stencils from wax paper and later introduced copper-plate engraving. Houston travelled to Japan in 1958 and to Paris in 1961 in order to expand upon his knowledge of print-making techniques.

15 Martijn, op. cit., 563.

16 See, for example, James A. Houston, "Contemporary Art of the Eskimo" in *The Studio* (February 1954) and Houston, *Canadian Eskimo Art* published by the Department of Northern Affairs and National Resources (Ottawa 1954).

17 Houston, op. cit., *Canadian Eskimo Art,* 38.

18 James A. Houston, "Eskimo Carvings," mimeograph of an article printed in *Craft Horizons* in April 1954 then reprinted in *Northern Affairs Bulletin,* vol. 5, no. 2 (March 1958), 1.

19 For a discussion of this theme see Jacqueline Delange Fry, "Contemporary Arts in Non-western Societies," *Arts Canada* (December 1971/January 1972), 96–101.

20 Bob Barnabas cited in Susan Cowan, ed., *We Don't Live in Snow Houses Now; Reflections of Arctic Bay* (Ottawa 1976), 134.

21 Ibid., 159.

22 David Ippirq recalled looking at George Swinton's *Sculpture of the Eskimo* (New York 1962) and finding that the sculptures "were not well made," Cowan, op. cit., 139.

23 Dorothy Eber, "Looking for the Artists of Dorset" in "Eskimo Art" *Canadian Forum,* vol. 52, no. 618–619 (July-August 1972), 14.

24 CGCQ, James Houston, "Eskimo Handicrafts: a Private Guide for the Hudson's Bay Company Manager" 1953, 4.

25 James Houston, *Eskimo Prints* (Barrie, Mass. 1971), 18, 21.

26 National Archives of Canada, RG85, vol. 387, File 255–5/166 [1], James Houston, "Excerpt from Monthly Report, 26 April 1957."

27 Eber, op. cit.

28 Cowan, op. cit., 119.

29 Av Isaacs, "On Dealing in Eskimo Art," *Canadian Forum,* vol. 52, no. 618–619 (July-August 1972), 19.

30 Graburn, op. cit., 137.

31 Peter Pitseolak cited in Dorothy Eber, *People from Our Side: A Life Story with Photographs by Peter Pitseolak* (Edmonton 1975), 145.

32 George Swinton, "The Changing Art of the Eskimo," in *Eskimo Sculpture,* The Winnipeg Art Gallery (Winnipeg 1967), 34.

33 Isaacs, op. cit., 16.

34 Penny Petrone, ed., *Northern Voices, Inuit Writing in English* (Toronto 1988), 180.

35 Blodgett, op. cit., 36.

36 Martijn, op. cit., 583.

37 Edmund Carpenter, *Eskimo Realities* (New York 1972), 194, 200.

38 Charles Gimpel, *The Canadian Eskimo in a Changing World,* Gimpel Fils Gallery (London December 1961), n.p.

39 William Gaunt, "Eskimo Culture Survives," *Sunday Telegraph* (London), 24 December 1961.

40 Gimpel, op. cit., *The Canadian Eskimo in a Changing World.*

41 GFGA, "Clipping files," *The Sunday Times,* 17 December 1961, praised the "beautiful photographs" and the art work as giving "a remarkably vivid and, indeed haunting idea both of life in the Arctic and of the persistence of the artistic impulse in even the most unfavourable conditions."

42 GFGA, Gimpel to W.E. Taylor, 17 November 1964.

43 Gimpel arranged this through the Department of Northern Affairs and Natural Resources in 1962. See GFGA, Charles Gimpel to R.A.J. Phillips Assistant Director of the Department of Northern Affairs and Natural Resouces, 2 February 1962. Also see ibid.,

R.G. Robertson, Deputy Minister of Northern Affairs and Natural Resources, 16 April 1962.

44   GFGA, Charles Gimpel to Kay Gimpel, 4/5 May 1961.

PART THREE

1   GFGA, Untitled and incomplete essay or lecture [1964], 8 typed pages.

2   Ibid.

3   GFGA, Charles Gimpel to Malvina Balus, Hudson's Bay Company, Winnipeg, 4 December 1964.

4   GFGA, Lorne Smith, "Preliminary Survey of Enukso Point Site, Fox Peninsula, NWT" [1968].

5   B.W. Lewis, "Inukshuks and Inuguaks" *Canadian Geographical Journal* (September 1966), 85.

6   GFGA, Charles Gimpel to Terry Ryan, 30 December 1964. It should be noted that in 1961 Terry Ryan shipped two Inuksuiit to Ontario for display at the airport in Toronto.

7   Gimpel's Inuksuk now stands at the entrance to the Scott Polar Research Institute in Cambridge, England.

8   Houston, op. cit., author's interview.

9   Author's interview with Terry Ryan, 9 June 1993.

10   GFGA, Charles Gimpel to "Allie" [Alma Houston], 30 December 1964.

11   GFGA has a good collection of these reviews.

12   GFGA, op. cit., Gimpel to "Allie."

13   Ibid.

PART FOUR

1   GFGA, untitled, undated, incomplete essay by Charles Gimpel [1964].

2   Richard W. Butler, "How To Control It – Snow-mobiles," *Canadian Geographical Journal,* vol. 88, no. 23 (March 1974), 5.

3   Susan Cowan, ed. *We Don't Live in Snow Houses Now; Reflections of Arctic Bay* (Ottawa 1976), 61.

4   Hugh Brody, "Alcohol, Change and the Industrial Frontier," *Inuit Studies,* vol. 1, no. 2 (1977), 42.

5   National Archives of Canada, see RG18 85–86, volume 366, for RCMP reports.

6   Dorothy Eber, *People from Our Side: A Life Story with Photographs by Peter Pitseolak* (Edmonton 1975), 148.

7   Cowan, op. cit., 175.

8   Mary Crnkovich, ed., *"Gossip" A Spoken History of Women in the North* (Ottawa 1990), 20.

9   Ibid.

10   By the early 1970s the arts income of Cape Dorset's population of six hundred was over a million dollars a year. The total Inuit arts income from all communities was about six million dollars. David Damas, *Arctic, Handbook of North American Indians,* vol. 5 (Washington 1984), 668.

11   Both Kenojuak and Parr had received the Order of Canada by 1968.

12   Okpik, "What Does It Mean To Be Eskimo?" *North,* vol. IX, no. 2 (March/April 1962), 28.

13   National Library of Canada, James Houston Papers, Box 50, "Introduction" [typescript] n.p.

14   W.C. Sturtevant, "The First Inuit Depiction by Europeans," *Inuit Studies,* vol. 4, no 1–2 (1980), 47–50.

15   Alma Houston, "Introduction," *Inuit Art* (Winnipeg 1988), 10.

16   GFGA, Kay Gimpel to Alice Houston, 5 August 1973.

17   Robert McKenzie, "Address" Memorial Chapel Service, Grosvenor Chapel, 15 February 1973.

INDEX